Smart Women

Don't

Get Wrinkles

LOOK AND FEEL 10 YEARS YOUNGER
WITHOUT EFFORT

Helena Frith Powell

GIBSON SQUARE

helenafrithpowell.com

Also available by Helena Frith Powell:

Love in a Warm Climate (fiction)
The Ex Factor (fiction)
Two Lipsticks and a Lover
Ciao Bella
More More France

This edition published for the first time by Gibson Square in 2017

UK   Tel: +44 (0)20 7096 1100
US   Tel: +1 646 216 9488

   rights@gibsonsquare.com
   www.gibsonsquare.com

   ISBN 9781783340910

Printed by CPI.

Introduction

For my mother,
who would rather have laughter lines than Botox

Introduction

It was when I was driving and I caught sight of myself in my rear view mirror that I first realised I was ageing. There was a crisscross of wrinkles across my forehead and around my eyes. In between my eyebrows there was a great big dip, which made me look permanently angry. I felt that sort of pit-of-the-stomach horror you have when something hideous happens.

Of course it hadn't happened overnight, but I had been so busy raising five small children (two step-children and three of my own) that I hadn't really focused on myself for some time. At the time of my discovery my smallest one was four and so at school in the mornings. I finally had time to look in the mirror. I tried to reason that the light was harsh, but there was no getting away from the image staring back at me.

My mother, who is in her early seventies, uses a different yardstick: 'You know you're getting old when your toy-boys start hitting 40,' she said to me the other day. She has completely grey hair, wrinkles, but looks great. She is still slim, moves well and has a glint in her eye. I think she could have had less wrinkles, if she'd ever bothered to use a sun screen or even a moisturizer, but she is the kind of woman who really doesn't do all that sort of stuff and is happy with the way she looks. She is the quintessential hippy; entirely carefree and has never owned any property in her life (way too risky!). Don't get me wrong; she has not let herself go à la Brigitte Bardot, but she hasn't done anything to actively slow the ageing process down except for eating well and practicing yoga. And obviously indulging in the odd toy-boy.

A rich aunt of mine, who often tries to pass herself off as my sister, however, is the polar opposite to both my mother and Bardot. She is older than the two of them but still wears haute-couture knee-high leather boots. Her hair is dyed jet black, her lips are plumped (sadly she had the treatment very early on and as a result is stuck with a permanent trout-pout, just like Emmanuelle Béart), and she spends more on skin creams a week than my mother has during her lifetime. It takes her hours to get ready in the mornings, but no one would guess her real age. They would, however, see that she is an older woman trying to look younger.

And that is not what this book is going to help you do. This book is going to help you look younger without anyone noticing that you're trying to do so. What I like to aim for is somewhere in between my aunt who can afford any treatment and has practically tried them all and my mother who would much rather spend her money on a good book than on even the tiniest squirt of Botox. Of course all women get wrinkles, even smart ones. But the smart ones can work out ways to avoid too many wrinkles, and will also use other tricks to look good without spending a fortune. Not just in looks, but in attitude, the way they move and the way they live.

By experiencing treatments at expensive health clinics, being a guinea pig for therapies like the vampire facial, interviewing scientists at cosmetic laboratories and universities, and those whose day job it is to make us look good, such as hairdressers, beauticians and beauty journalists, I have discovered the key areas that we need to focus on to stay attractive for longer, a sort of top tips to look younger with treatments that don't cost the earth. If you'd like to know what they are, then read on...

What age group are these tips for? I am no longer so sure after writing this book and meeting the experts. Ingeborg van Lotringen, *Cosmopolitan* Beauty Director, says that she receives a lot of questions about wrinkles from readers in their early twenties. And one Cambridge scientist you will meet later on even thinks you should start prevention in the womb! Whatever else, I hope you will enjoy the book and get something out of the tips. If you change one thing in your life that makes you look or feel better, then I have achieved what I set out to do.

In addition, at the end of the chapters are the details sections, high-lighting in-depth the things I tried and which I am most persuaded by — and which I am now following myself!

1

The future is fat

'I believe in loyalty: I think when a woman reaches an age she likes she should stick with it.'
Eva Gabor

You wait all your life for a decent plastic surgeon, then two identical ones come along at once.

'I would give you some Botox, yes, I can see while you are talking that you have some movement and you need some Botox,' says Dr Roberto Viel, co-founder and Plastic Surgeon at the London Centre for Aesthetic Surgery. 'And in my opinion you need to build up this part there and there,' he continues, grabbing my cheekbones. 'It's getting a little bit too flat. And probably a little more definition and volume on the lips but just a little, I don't like too much. And then some fat or filler around the naso-labial folds. And also I would remove the excess skin on your eyelids. It's a simple operation.'

His twin brother Maurizio chips in 'I wouldn't add anything there,' he says pointing at my cheekbones, 'but here we need to use some filler.' He touches my face just above my jaw. 'I would also use a Dermalen mask as you have some skin pigmentation issues.'

I am visiting what I assume are the world's only plastic surgeon twins. They have offices in Dubai and London's Harley Street. I arrive at their Dubai office to see what they can do to help me in my anti-ageing quest.

The office is in Dubai's Healthcare City, a place where I guess you can have almost anything done from laser eye surgery to hair removal to breast enlargements. The city is divided into districts, buildings and blocks, all identical, all with a different treatment behind the door. I am in district 1, building 64, block E.

I arrive at suite 1604 and ring the bell. The door buzzes open and I am shown into one of two waiting rooms by a pretty receptionist. The separate rooms are a nice touch I feel. You don't really want to run into any acquaintances while you're here. No one visits the twins for a friendly chat. You come here because you need some work done. Serious anti-ageing work.

But I didn't realise quite how much I needed done until they told me. In fact, they would do more if I were able to stay for a few weeks. Such as harvest my fat, but more of that later.

Roberto and Maurizio were born in Milan to an opera singer mother and industrialist father. 'Our father was in plywood and timber and he wanted us to carry on the family business,' explains Roberto. 'But my mother wanted us to become doctors. She was more or less a hypochondriac so there were doctors around all the time. Our best family friend was a surgeon. So medicine was always present.'

What an Italian *mamma* wants, an Italian *mamma* gets. The twins studied medicine at the University of Milan and then went to London to specialise in plastic surgery. 'Plastic surgery felt like the field that was most appropriate for us,' explains Roberto. 'We grew up in an artistic environment with a mother who wanted to look good. And the ability to rejuvenate and improve defects in people and help them to stay younger was most appealing. We liked the idea of going into something medical but that was still related to beauty.'

Roberto is wearing a surgical shirt with a surfing motif. The matching skullcap sits on the desk in front of him. His brother is wearing a chic blue and white stripy shirt. They both wear a pair of red glasses you can unclip at the front that hang around their necks when they're not peering at my face. They are tall, slim and handsome, with thick dark hair and firm jawlines. I know they are 50 years old from my research and am tempted to ask if they give each other the odd injection from time to time, just to make sure they look closer to 40. If they do, they must coordinate it very well. They really are utterly identical. Even down to their gorgeous Italian accents. It's uncanny. I ask them if they have ever tricked a difficult patient who insists on seeing one of them by sending the other one along if they're not free. 'We used to do that with girlfriends,' laughs Roberto. 'But never with patients.'

After completing their studies the brothers opened up a practice in Harley Street in 1990. They made their name using a pioneering technique of liposuction and also 'enlarging manhoods' as Maurizio puts it. Apparently they have enlarged 'thousands' of them.

It was at the behest of Middle Eastern clients that they opened up a second office in Dubai in 2008. 'That way we could provide consistency in treatment for them,' says Maurizio. 'I moved here full time in 2006 to oversee the building works and the opening and stayed here. Roberto is now here much more too, but he goes to London for one week every month.'

I ask if there is a lot of sibling rivalry between them, especially now that they're working together most of the time. 'There is always competition between us, has been since we were young children, in high school and at university but it was a healthy competition to push us and to achieve the best we could,' says Roberto. 'It was positive competition,' adds Maurizio.

So what is the future of anti-ageing? I moot the theory that in a few years' time women will no longer go under the knife because the methods we have using lasers and such tools will be so sophisticated.

Roberto shakes his head. 'There will always be a need for surgery. Non-surgical treatments have limits,' he says. 'Of course there are many ways we can slow down skin laxity but the only thing that can remove excess of sagging skin is surgery.'

Maurizio agrees: 'Non-surgical treatments can slow down and delay the need for more invasive treatments. And surgery of the future will be less invasive and there will be less down-time and minimal scars. But the perfect doctor has to be able to offer both surgical and non-surgical skills. The two things will always be together. Non-surgical can delay things but there will be a time when the surgical has to come to the party.'

In terms of non-surgical treatments, what do they rate as the most effective?

'Botox is one of the most beneficial and effective in anti-ageing because it gets to the cause of lines and wrinkles on the upper part of the face,' says Roberto. 'But for the future your own fat will be your best weapon for anti-ageing because we can use it to volumise the face instead of a filler.'

This is not new, LCAS have been doing it for more than 20 years, but there have been advances. Fat is rich in stem cells, for example, and can be used for all manner of anti-ageing tricks.

'If we put fat under your skin, your complexion will improve,' says Roberto. 'That is why it is much more effective than the man-made fillers such as Juvederm or Restalyne.'

Roberto describes fat as 'the next generation of anti-ageing tool' because of the enormous amount of potential it has. Working with a lab in Dubai they have started to cultivate clients' fat for skin rejuvenation and augmentation. For example, my nasty wrinkle down the side of my face would be a perfect victim for Dr Roberto's fat treatment.

'A filler is a quick fix,' adds Maurizio, 'for when you don't have time to collect your fat, but if you want to be more comprehensive and gain more in the long run your own fat is the best. That's why keeping a little fat in the body is always beneficial.'

They explain that fat is very rich in growth factors, and when activated it stimulates the production of new blood vessels, which bring more oxygen and nutrients to the skin that ultimately translate in the production of new collagen. Of course collagen is the substance that keeps our skin plump and young looking. And as we age, we lose it. Fat is also extremely rich in stem cells, famous for their rejuvenating potential, and the absolute buzzword in anti-ageing. Stem cells are so exciting because of their regenerative powers. In medicine in general they may soon be used to treat everything from blindness to cancer, but in terms of more cosmetic use they are already playing a huge role in the kinds of treatments dermatologists and plastic surgeons like the Viel twins can offer. The reason they are so important is that they are a bit like building blocks for your skin; they have the ability to replace damaged cells, thus regenerating your skin. Basically they are let loose (once injected) and go about their job of healing automatically.

I ask them what clients are looking for nowadays, what has changed in the 20 years since they started their practice.

'They want maximum results with minimum downtime,' says Maurizio. 'For example we no longer do strong peels, which we used to get very good results from, but patients just can't take a week to recover nowadays and the effect was a bit traumatic for patients. And they don't want any scars at all, so keyhole surgery is becoming more and more advanced.'

'They want something that looks natural, that doesn't look like they've had anything done, but just like they've been on holiday,' adds Roberto.

We are ready for my treatment. Botox first. Roberto does the honours. 'Do you like to keep some movement?'

'Yes I think so.'

He explains that the problem with that is you can get some wrinkles just above your eyebrows. OK, let's go for no movement. Roberto asks me to frown and to smile and puts little dots where he is going to inject me.

'A little scratch,' he warns me as the first needle goes in. It is a little scratch. Not pleasant but not terribly painful either.

Next up is Maurizio who studies my face with his eyes and his hands. He reminds me of a sculptor planning his masterpiece. He also covers my face in dots to show where the needle will go. While he injects me, Roberto holds bits of cotton swab where his brother has just inserted the filler. He strokes my head and tells me how well I'm doing. I feel like a Hollywood A-list star in the hands of both twins at once. And strangely enough, considering one of them still has a needle in his hand, I feel very safe.

'And the lips?' asks Roberto as Maurizio finishes my face.

'I won't do the lips today,' he says.

I am between relieved and rather disappointed. Much as I fear the dreaded 'trout pout' I have always felt my lips are a bit, well, puny really. But what Maurizio says goes. I get the impression he is the boss in the pairing and it comes as no surprise when he tells me he was born first.

The twins lead me to the mirror to admire their handiwork. The Botox will not show for several days, but the fillers already show. I have a few red bits from the needle, which don't look great, but on the whole my face looks a lot perkier. I look more alert, more alive, younger I guess is the only way to put it. And funnily enough, happier. One of the effects of ageing is that everything in your face droops, which inevitably makes you look miserable. Maurizio has lifted it all in a matter of minutes. But they insist my own fat would be more effective.

'Keep some fat,' Roberto urges me as I say goodbye. 'We will use it to very good effect.'

Maurizio nods in agreement. 'Eat some pasta.'

I have just met a woman with a fat-melting machine who promises to remove any middle-aged spread I have, but I will of course keep some fat for the twins. How can I possibly resist?

As you will see at the end of this chapter, I didn't.

Skin Deep

What I tried: Meso Vytal Micro Needling. A machine that injects highly effective serums into your skin and also promotes the production of collagen.

What I expected: I thought it would be painful, as it involves needles, but also effective. I work on the 'no pain, no gain' principle when it comes to anti-ageing treatments. The blurb promised rejuvenation, a slowing down of wrinkles and an instant glow.

What happened: The treatment begins with a mild (five per cent) aha peel. This prepares the skin for the needles and the serums that will be applied. It is true that most skin treatments use products that sit on the surface of the skin, and 20 per cent or less will be absorbed. So although it was painful in places (around the eyes and the forehead mainly), I was prepared to stand the pain so that the Meso Vytal ingredients could penetrate the area between my epidermis and dermis. My therapist worked all over my face and neck, telling me she was going to go over problem areas twice or more times. Apparently this one of the few treatments that can make a difference to your neck, which is lucky because mine is beginning to look like a turkey's.

Wrinkles, or wrinkle free? I looked extremely fresh afterwards, which was miraculous as I had been out partying until 2am the night before. It is definitely a beauty, but I would suggest a course of at least eight treatments in total to get the full benefits of it. This is, I think, the way the future of semi-invasive anti-ageing treatments are going. Not as violent as the knife, but they can get under the surface of the skin and really make a difference.

Don't try this at home

Meeting the plastic-fantastic twins made me realise how careful you have to be when entrusting your looks to relative strangers. For example, I had a lovely dermatologist in Abu Dhabi I used to go to for facials and the like. One day I complained about the wrinkle that runs down the side of my face, which she said she could get rid of with a filler injection. She duly did so, removing at least half of the wrinkle, what joy, but at the same time she created an imbalance in my face, that I wasn't even aware of until Maurizio pointed it out to me. And this is a professional. She also put fillers just under my mouth, I think in an effort to lift it, but I ended up with two little pouches instead. I looked a bit like a hamster. So don't go for Botox with a dentist who isn't trained in dermatology. Don't be seduced by special offers from places that spring up on the High Street. Nothing looks cheaper or uglier than work badly done and it could be permanent. Just remember what happened to the beautiful Emmanuelle Béart who starred in Manon de Sources and was possibly the most stunning woman in the world until at the age of 27 when she had her lips done — badly. Sadly for her this was in pre-filler days and the surgery she had is permanent. She is now a vocal opponent of plastic surgery.

2

Pumping fat

'Grow fat and look young.'
John Dryden

There are certain times in your life when you wonder what you are doing and why. As I lie on an operating table at the London Centre for Aesthetic Surgery in Harley Street I have one of those moments.

There is a kindly nurse holding my hand as a plastic surgeon pushes a thin metal rod repeatedly into my abdomen through a small incision he has made in my stomach. In the background there is rap music blaring from a radio. Can it get any worse?

What's really extraordinary is that I'm here voluntarily. I am not being cured of some nasty disease, or undergoing a life-saving operation. I am here for a treatment known as Facial Stem Cell Rejuvenation. This has nothing to do with health and everything to do with curiosity. Is it really possible to trick your cells into turning back the clock? I am lying here like a piece of meat on a slab undergoing a minor operation in order to look younger. Have I finally gone mad?

As a beauty writer, I am not unused to anti-ageing treatments. I have tried everything from the pedestrian such as

Botox to the totally nuts like the Vampire Facial (more on that below). But this is the most drastic thing I have ever done. And it is the very latest thing in anti-ageing. I first heard about it when I was researching the book, but it took me a while to pluck up the courage to actually try it.

The idea behind it is that you stimulate the skin's own ability to repair itself by injecting fresh stem cells into it, which encourage it to produce collagen and elastin. The damaged skin cells that cause fine lines, wrinkles and all those things that age us will be outnumbered by new, healthy cells that will go to work, rejuvenating my skin by restoring lost volume, as well as improving the complexion and reducing wrinkles.

But as I lie there having my stomach rather vigorously pumped for fat, I wonder if I will end up wrinkle-free and gorgeous, or will I just look like a mad woman with part of her stomach on her face?

The fat harvesting is the first stage of a process that will take around six weeks in total. The reason they use fat is that it is particularly rich in stem cells, the magical ingredient that will restore me to my younger self. Once the fat is harvested, it is sent away to some lab where the cells are extracted and treated to ensure they will live on to do their repair work once re-injected.

No one has really said much about this part of the treatment, although I was told to take Arnica for a week beforehand and avoid alcohol, both of which of course I have failed to do.

In my experience plastic surgeons always say there will be hardly or no effect on you when they go to work on you, and then there always is. I'm not quite sure what I expected when Dr Viel said he was going harvest fat from my stomach. I guess I just thought they would pop in a tube and suck it out. But this is a proper operation, that involves my surgeon and a nurse 'scrubbing in' (I love that phrase ever since Grey's Anatomy), me under local anaesthetic and covered in green surgical material. Dr Viel approaches me with the most enormous needle I have ever seen.

'Don't worry, it's the same kind as dentists use,' he reassures me. I'm not sure why that's meant to make me feel any better.

'You'll just feel a tiny scratch,' he says, pointing the needle up in the air and squirting some of the liquid out like a fountain. I daren't look as he inserts it into my swabbed, exposed stomach. Next up is the scalpel. He cuts a tiny slit in my flesh and then inserts what looks like a rather over-sized, thick knitting needle with holes in it. This is then poked and prodded around inside my stomach. It lasts about a minute and a half.

That wasn't too bad I think.

'Now we wait,' he says settling down in a chair next to me.

'For what?'

'For the anaesthetic to take effect.'

'You mean that wasn't the fat harvesting?'

Dr Viel chuckles. 'No, that was the anaesthetic going in.'

In fact there is a lot more to come. After about ten minutes Dr Viel sticks the metal tube back into my stomach and asks me if I can feel anything.

It is slightly reminiscent of the Caesarean I had with my middle child. You can feel something going on, but it doesn't hurt. Dr Viel pushes the over-grown knitting needle back and forth energetically.

The rap music has now been replaced with Jack Johnson, which slightly relaxes me. At the end of about 20 minutes (but it feels like much longer) Dr Viel proudly shows me two vials of what looks like blood mixed with fat. I try to look suitably impressed.

'Is it enough?' I ask him. I am really not keen on more harvesting. I feel a bit like I've been beaten up.

'Yes,' he smiles, handing the vials over to his nurse to be labelled.

Dr Viel stitches me up (OK only the one stitch). It does occur to me that I have had a minor operation. Once the stitch is in Dr Viel straps tape extremely tightly over my stomach. I am told I need to leave this on for three days.

I get dressed and notice that the tight tape that is pushing my poor swollen stomach into a Michelin-style tyre. My stomach is not yet sore but I know it will be by the time I get home. It is, and it remains sore for several days, as well as extremely bruised and rather unattractive. Should have taken that Arnica…

Phase two of the treatment involves the injections and takes place three weeks after the harvesting. This time I am in the hands of Dr Roberto Viel, the twin brother of Maurizio Viel who removed my fat, both of whom I have met several times in Dubai. It's impossible to tell the difference between them. I ask Roberto if they ever stand in for each other with patients. They don't, he tells me. But they used to with girlfriends.

A nurse covers my face in a cream that will slightly numb it. I am quite proud of my pain threshold and smugly think I won't need it. How wrong I am. Today's process has two main components. The first is the preparation whereby Dr Viel runs what is called a derma roller all over my face to create hundreds of tiny incisions that will receive the stem cells. The second part is the actual injection of stem cells using an extremely thin needle. Both parts are bloody painful, especially on the bonier parts of the face. I can feel the liquid pouring down the side of my face and I hate to think of it being wasted on my ears. Dr Viel rubs the excess into my skin. After about 45 minutes it's finished. The nurse covers my skin in a heavenly serum called Dr Viel's X118 Intense Hydrating Serum that is one of the most soothing things I have ever felt. My face is by now really sore and I look in the mirror rather hesitatingly, dreading what

I will look like. Actually I have a deep healthy red glow that is approaching a tomato, or sunburn, but not terrible. My face does feel like it's been burned; it is tight, uncomfortable, sore, vulnerable and raw.

The following day I look like I've been punched in both eyes and a series of rather dramatic grazes have appeared all over my face. I look, well to be honest, extremely old and rather sad. The worst bits are under my eyes, which are rubbed raw. Imagine a combination of constant crying, being punched in the eyes, incessant rubbing and an eye infection and you get the general impression. I am endlessly applying Dr Viel's soothing serum in the hope that it will magically smooth it all away. It is a gorgeous serum, supremely moisturizing, and glides on like silk. It does help, but nothing can disguise the damage. (It costs £35, and is sold at the clinic if you're interested, a lot cheaper than the main brands and much better in my opinion).

This is what is called 'down-time' in the industry. That is the time that you can't be seen in public because you look like a lunatic. The problem is it coincides with the end of term and I have all sorts of things I need to go to such as the mothers' and sons' tennis tournament, the fathers' and sons' cricket match and the school drinks party.

'Do I look like I've been punched in both eyes?' I ask my husband as we prepare to leave for one of the events.

'Pretty much,' he replies.

I wear enormous dark glasses for the next four days, even when it's raining, which is most of the time. After that the scratches and bruising disappear. Ten days later I notice that my skin is glowing. Two weeks after the injections I have to collect someone from the airport and get to bed at 3am. The next morning I head to the bathroom and half open my eyes to look in the mirror. I expect to see a gaunt, exhausted face staring back at me. Instead I see a fresh-faced person who looks like she went to bed at 10pm. Incredible. I remember the first Dr Viel saying to me that once it kicks in I will be able to go out without putting any make-up on because the quality of my skin will be so much better. I am pleasantly surprised by the difference. My skin looks moist, healthy, clear and above all, young. And what's amazing is that the treatment will keep on improving for weeks. It won't even reach its absolute best for another month or so. It also lasts for several years, depending of course on your lifestyle.

So I don't plan on staying up until 3am every night, but when I do, I know I will wake up looking like I haven't.

www.lcas.com

3

The psychic Dyson

'The part can never be well unless the whole is well.'
Plato

'You were a Cathar,' he tells me. 'I remember you. You were burned at the stake.' If Simon is right, I have aged incredibly well. The Cathars were around between the 12th and 14th centuries.

I have come to visit Simon as his reputation is spreading as a holistic healer with an ability to reverse (at best) or slow down (at worst) the ageing process. His elegant, expensive office is in the heart of Marylebone in London and when you walk in you are hit by a smell that is hard to define but is somewhere between incense and lemongrass room spray. The walls are an extremely Zen pale olive green, the furniture grey, the floors and doors all polished wood.

I am feeling slightly wounded by the more traditional anti-ageing methods. My latest round of anti-ageing research (more details later!) for this book has left me with a black vein on my forehead that doesn't look like it will ever go away and raw skin around my eyes. In other words I am in the mood for some alternative anti-ageing and do not run screaming for the hills when Simon announces that he knew me as a Cathar.

On some levels he is the kind of man my husband would call a quack. In fact, quite a lot of people would call him a quack, or even a witch doctor, but he seems somehow too grounded to be either. He is nice looking, with a great aura (yep I already picked up a bit of the lingo), trendily dressed in a black shirt, jeans and purple Converse trainers. He's also an ardent Arsenal fan, which of course makes him questionable to a Chelsea fan, but you don't get many football fans parading as witch doctors.

My first question is how he can possibly reverse the ageing process.

He laughs. 'I told you reversing ageing is possible, I didn't say I could tell you how! But actually it's all about entropy, the decline of the body from an ordered state into a chaotic state. What we need to do is to restore the ordered state.'

Simon believes he can restore the ordered state with a combination of Reiki (he is a Reiki master), light therapy and physic surgery. The basic concept is to eliminate blockages. Blockages are what cause stress, illness and ageing. You can compare it to the skin on your face. If you don't cleanse it, your pores get clogged up and the dirt left there eventually creates oxidation, which damages the skin. If your body is not cleansed, and the meridians left blocked, the blockages get worse and worse, resulting in all sorts of symptoms, ageing being just one of them.

'We have 144 meridians,' Simon explains, 'but the most crucial one runs right through the middle of your body from your head (the crown chakra) to the root chakra. Think of it like a train-line from London to Glasgow. There are permeations off to other places all the way up, but if that line is blocked, nothing else works.'

If you can't visit Simon there is a way to get your main meridian flowing. You do what is known as pumping the Hu

Yim. Those of you of a delicate disposition look away now. You basically press the tip of your tongue against the roof of your mouth 2/3 of a centimetre behind your teeth. While you are pushing your tongue back and forth you also contract your pelvic floor muscles.

'I do it all the time,' says Simon. 'It was as if I had struck gold when I discovered it. I haven't been ill since. And no one I have told about it has been ill either. And I'm not a saint, I go to the pub, I drink beer I have all the stresses that goes with having four children and a busy life.'

Simon's argument is that you can do Botox and use expensive creams and all those things will work, but if you're not looking after the root of the issue, that is your body as a whole, then you will age more rapidly than you need to.

'People come and see me before they have photo shoots because they leave here looking ten years younger,' he says. And although he is a holistic practitioner he is well aware of the cosmetic benefits of the light therapy he uses.

'My partner Charlotte is an actress and uses the lasers a lot. In fact she did an experiment once where she used the laser on one hand and not on the other. The difference after just three days was really noticeable.'

But he emphasizes that the de-stressing of a patient plays just as big a part. 'You know when you come back from holiday and everyone tells you how marvellous you look? Well of course it may be in part due to the fact that you have a tan, but it's also because you've de-stressed. Stress is the biggest killer. When you get stressed your body goes into flight mode, it shuts down, and gets blocked. So it is unable to process toxins or information or heal in a natural flow as it should be doing.'

His advice for de-stressing, as well as pumping the Hu Yim, is to lessen your dependency on people and things. 'We need to learn to plug into a universal energy and not rely on people or things so much. Imagine you and I are sitting in an orchard and we each have a basket of apples. I decide to take one of your apples. Now why would I do that when we are surrounded by trees with fruit? Sure we all want certain things, but don't waste all your power and energy in craving or thinking you won't be happy until you have a certain job or a certain person falls in love with you. Be more self reliant, it will decrease your stress levels immediately.'

Simon sees ageing as something that is in the mind. 'We are programmed to think, 'Oh I'm 60, I must be getting old.' But this is so wrong. Why do we live our lives according to some programme? Ageing is as much a mindset as anything else. I have a new client who is 80. This lady had a really tough life and a couple of months ago she just decided she wanted a real change, she wanted to transform her life into something else and she wanted to look younger. She's great and we've been working hard together and the difference is incredible. Age should not be a barrier. Why don't more people see it as an opportunity?'

Simon suggests we spend an hour opening my chakras and unblocking years of angst and stress. 'Your cells are like a cake tin with a cut in it. Even though they renew, they pass the memory of traumatic incidents on to the new cells. My aim to cleanse them now, to give your body a chance to flow.'

This is not as simple (or as painless) as it may sound. The first thing he does is touch my feet. Agony.

'Do you have problems with your back?' I do. 'Digestion?' Yep. The two-hour treatment is rather like reflexology times 100. At times I don't think I can stand it any longer. It literally is as close to torture as I have ever come. Images of what I think must have gone on in Pinochet's torture chambers flood into my mind. And the life-size red candle skull behind my head doesn't help. But Simon insists it's necessary. That we have to get rid of all those years of angst, trauma and stress, we need to re-cut the cookie tin.

I guess I have enough faith in him to let him carry on. Added to which, it is quite compelling to believe that someone has the power to remove all my demons and allow me to start again, cleansed and pure, ready for the rest of my life. And of course if it hurts this much, it must be doing some good.

'Think of me as a psychic Dyson,' says Simon. 'Sucking out all the trauma and damage from your past.' He stands behind my head and puts his hands around my face. He then invokes the masters from the past to assist us in this cleansing and purifying process. I do wonder then whether he's a bit of a nutter. But the diagnosis he makes when it comes to where I have pain and problems is so spot on that I do believe he really is on to something. And I'm not even sure he needs to invoke the past masters to help him.

I do feel different after the treatment, lighter somehow and the pains in my back disappear for a couple of weeks. I would think a holistic treatment like Simon's needs regular top-ups if it's really going to have an effect on you. But I suppose that's like any treatment, whether it is expensive or of the home-remedy variety.

There is something to be said for holistic anti-ageing methods, which I guess is why week-long spa breaks are such a lovely idea because you not only have the treatments but also the time to relax and de-stress. Stress is one of the most ageing things there is, and the annoying thing is that as we age we produce less DHEA, which is a hormone that protects us from the stress hormone cortisol.

'By the time you're about 70 you only make 10 per cent of the DHEA you made when you were 30,' says Professor Janet Lord, Director of the MRC-ARUK Centre for Musculoskeletal

Ageing Research at the University of Birmingham. 'And at the same time, unfortunately, your ability to create cortisol is retained.'

So a kind of seriously stressful double whammy. As Dr Anna Phillips, a Reader in Behavioural Medicine at Birmingham University who has conducted award-winning research on stress notes, 'ageing is like a massively long, slow stress response.' Professor Lord says there are plans afoot to produce the anti-stress hormone in tablet form. 'We know it works in animals,' she says. 'If we give them DHEA they recover from trauma and injury much better.'

But until that tablet is available, we need to learn how to deal with stress, or better still, avoid it. In 2012 a study was published that concluded that stress could have a harmful effect on our telomeres. If you imagine a shoelace and the end bit that keeps that lace intact, the telomeres are the end bits of our DNA. Once they go, the lace starts to fray. This is what happens to our cells, when the telomeres get shorter (which they can do due to stress) the cells can die or become damaged. And ageing cells are of course at the root of ageing. Stress also ages the brain, accelerating the onset of diseases such as Alzheimer's. Rather depressingly some research suggests that women's brains age faster than men's due to the fact that women are more affected by stress.

And of course the more we stress the more we do unhealthy things to compensate for the stress such as drinking too much alcohol and caffeine, not exercising and eating the wrong things. Our sleep can also be badly affected by stress, which in turn leads to more stress.

Another factor that makes us stressed is social isolation. According to Professor Lord over one million adults in the UK live three hours away from their nearest relative. 'And half a million old people have not spoken to anybody in a month.

Being socially isolated is extremely stressful, it raises cortisol levels and causes depression. And of course with reduced levels of DHEA, which is an anti-depressant, we can't counterbalance the high levels of cortisol. So that expression 'grumpy old man' actually has some physiological truth to it.'

Clearly ageing well is about more than the right face cream. There has to be a holistic element to it that balances you in other ways than a facial or a cream can. Whether you get that holistic side from yoga, or mediation or walking or visiting people like the Psychic Dyson is up to you. Professor Lynn Cox from the University of Oxford, a leading authority on senescent cells and how they affect us, said several times during our meeting (Chapter nine has more advice from her): 'Don't ever forget the mindfulness.' What goes on in our mind is reflected in our bodies. You need to take good care of both.

Top Tip

To say that I am obsessed with pillows is an understatement. Whenever I travel, the first thing I pack is my pillow. When we lived in the Middle East and had maids making our beds I wrote my name on my pillow to ensure it didn't end up on my husband's side of the bed. If my Hungarian goose down pillow ever goes missing (unlikely as I've had it electronically tagged) I can't sleep. Then there's the pillow case. Much has been written about the benefits of a silk pillowcase, and how sleeping on anything else will make the wrinkles in your face deeper. I can only confirm that a silk pillowcase is an essential part of your beauty routine. But make sure it is 100 per cent silk, any man-made fibre will negate the benefits. There's a time to save and a time to spend: this is a time to spend. My pillow case comes from John Lewis and costs £40, cheaper than an anti-wrinkle cream and more effective. Obviously the most effective way to avoid wrinkles while you sleep is to sleep on your back, but I can rarely do that.

4

Face the facts
(and the neck)

*'Be on the alert to recognise your prime at whatever
time of your life it may occur.'*
Muriel Spark

I have my godson to thank for the revelation that was my Clarisonic cleansing brush. Not directly of course, he is lovely but at the age of 19 and with a penchant for strange music he is hardly aware of the sort of present that might make a godmother's heart melt. It was his mother who gave me the brush. Freddie came to stay with us for a month during his gap year. As a thank you his mother Rachel sent the most fabulous present along with him, a box filled with her favourite beauty products. There was some Eve Lom in there and some La Prairie. Rachel has never been one to economise when it comes to skincare. I remember once several years ago when my girls were toddlers and fond of playing with my face-creams she advised me to 'give them the cheap stuff, like your Clarins'.

Anyway, the parcel arrived with a note thanking for having Freddie to stay and explaining that 'this brush is the one thing I can honestly say has made the most dramatic difference to my skin of anything I have ever used'.

The concept of course makes sense. With a cleansing brush (they say it is six times more effective than cleansing with your hands) you are not only cleansing your skin but also removing dead skin cells, in effect a daily exfoliation.

Skin cells die and are replaced by new ones on the lower layers of the dermis. But as we get older our skin's regenerative powers get weaker, much like the rest of our regenerative powers. If you exfoliate regularly (which men do all the time when shaving) you can help your skin's regenerative process by removing the dead cells and making way for the new ones.

The other great thing about the Clarisonic is that you really do feel VERY clean after using it. Once you get used to it manual cleansing just isn't enough, although I do admit that there are times I'm too tired and the minute it takes (it has an automatic timer) seems like an hour.

For the utter cleansing fanatic there is also a larger stronger brush head you can use for your body. My friend gave me my brush with the face appliance for sensitive skin telling me the one for normal is too harsh. She is right, I tried it once and have gone back to the sensitive one. Another tip from a dermatologist I met is to take your make-up off before you use the brush, that way you really are getting a deep cleanse with no make-up being spread around your face. Clarisonic say this is not necessary, but then they would.

It's definitely worth investing in an electronic cleansing brush, or inviting some children of friends to stay in the hope they might bring one along.

There are several keys to great looking skin: eating well, sleeping well, staying hydrated, not stressing, but without a good cleansing regime, you will never have good or young looking skin. (Unless you are 13 years old, and then after a while you'll get acne.) Cleansing your skin needs to be a priority. One of the best tips I have heard during my months of research is to cleanse as soon as you get home. 'Don't leave it until you're ready to collapse into bed,' Ingeborg van Lotringen, Beauty Director of *Cosmopolitan Magazine* told me. 'Do it as soon as you get home and do it properly.'

There are so many benefits to cleansing, and so many downsides if you don't. On the positive side when you cleanse you:

* Remove toxins and impurities from the skin
* Remove dirt and make-up from the skin
* Remove dead skin
* Unclog pores
* Massage (stimulate) your skin
* Relax (if you do it when you're not exhausted that is)

On the negative side if you don't cleanse you:

* Increase the risks of premature ageing from external elements
* Will have impurities that will turn into free radicals and age your skin
* Will have dull skin tone
* Will have clogged up pores

According to Dr Nathalie Issachar, Global Director of Product Development for Clarins, around 75 per cent of visible side effects of skin ageing have to do with causes such as pollution and the sun, only 25 per cent are genetic.

Another top tip is to wash your hands before you start the cleansing process; otherwise you are just putting more dirt on your face before you even start. And as soon as that is done remove all eye make-up. Then you can start the serious business of cleansing. It is dull, and you need to do it twice a day (less thoroughly in the morning) and there will be times when you roll in at midnight and can't face it (pardon the pun). When this happens to me I use facial wipes, but on the whole I avoid them as they don't cleanse thoroughly enough.

If you can, have a facial once a month — either at home or in a spa. Start with the cleanser, then the exfoliator, then the mask. If I wake up with a hangover looking dreadful and can't really face doing much I sometimes give myself a mini-facial at home. It really brightens up your skin and also makes you forget your headache as you luxuriate in spending some time looking after your skin.

Obviously when I talk about cleansing the face, I am also including the neck area and décolletage. The latter is so often ignored, and you do so at your peril. As Cindy Crawford says; 'Women forget to take care of their décolletage and it shows their age.' Cindy uses the Meaningful Beauty range created by the Paris-based cosmetic doctor, Dr Sebagh.

I have lived in both the Middle East and the South of France where there are plenty of badly sun-damaged chests on view. These are women of a certain age who have clearly enjoyed plenty of long lunches in the sunshine, which is fine, and all very lovely, but it looks like they've forgotten to put their sunscreen on. The skin there is extremely delicate and damages very easily. Just try to get into the habit of treating your face, neck and décolletage as one area in terms of cleansing, moisturising and applying sunscreen.

I have never gone for any products specifically geared to my neck and décolletage. I don't see the point in spending more money on cosmetics than I have to, but, if you feel like splurging, both Sisley and Clarins do a lovely bust cream that you can rub all the way up to your neck.

In terms of the kind of cleanser to use, that will depend on four major factors. Your skin type, your age, whether you like to cleanse with or without water and your budget. One of the few upsides to getting older is that we usually have a bit more cash at our disposal so we can use more expensive products. Of course we NEED more expensive products as our skin ages. I use two main cleansers, the Eve Lom almost every day, and then the Malin+Goetz detox face mask as a bit of a change. I love the way it oxidises and tingles on my face, something they call amino acid hydration technology.

I find the Eve Lom cleanser is perfect for my skin type (dry and of a certain age), I love the smell and texture of it, and it does a great job. You just have to try lots of brands until you find the one you love. I much prefer cleansing with water, my skin doesn't really feel clean otherwise, and another old favourite is the Liz Earle Cleanse & Polish. It is quite similar to Eve Lom in that the idea is that you exfoliate with the muslin cloth and massage your skin. I of course also exfoliate with the Clarisonic brush, so am getting a double dose.

My daughters both started using a wash-off cleanser in their early teens and so far they have been spared the dreaded onset of adolescent spots. But more than avoiding spots, starting a skincare regime young is important because it sets you up for life with good habits. It also means your skin will be better prepared to face ageing. In your mid-twenties you should think about what anti-ageing products to start using. Elizabeth Arden has launched a brand called Flawless Future, aimed specifically at the 25-35 year old woman, and there are many more out there. The key to pinpointing which product will work for younger skin is to think light. You don't want to clog up your pores and your skin doesn't need the rich ingredients a woman's skin needs when no longer youthful. On the organic front I found Jurilique's Herbal Recovery Age Prevention line fabulous.

The non-surgical facelift

What I tried: The non-surgical facelift with threads by Dr Gabriela Mercik. A lift with surgical threads, large ones around the jaw and cheeks that literally lift your jawline and cheek area and then smaller ones throughout to lift bits here and there. An added benefit of these particular surgical threads (called Polydioxanone or PDO threads) is that they encourage the body to produce collagen, that holy grail of anti-ageing. I asked Dr Gabriela how this happens. 'We don't know,' she told me. 'It's magic.'

What I expected: This is one of those treatments I was always too scared to try until I met Dr Gabriela. The thought of someone sticking a large needle into my face and leaving a surgical thread under my skin didn't really appeal. It also seemed to me almost archaic and I just couldn't see how it would work. But Dr Gabriela insisted it would be just the thing for my sagging jawline. And then I met a lovely lady who had had the non-surgical facelift with Dr Gabriela and looks great, so I decided to go for it. I wasn't sure what to expect. Some pain for sure, and possibly a firmer jaw.

What happened? I sat for an hour and 20 minutes with some anaesthetic cream on in a small and extremely warm treatment room. After that I was taken up to Dr Gabriela's office and installed in the treatment chair. She injected me with more anaesthetic, each needle felt like a small electric shock. She inserted the first thread with a needle inside a canula. The whole process was reminiscent of liposuction, and I was surprised at how violent it was. The thread felt like it was slightly jagged. Once it was in, she twisted it, which is how the lift happens. She worked away with some smaller threads and then stepped back to admire her work. She was visibly thrilled. A mirror was given to me so I could see the difference between the two. It was undeniable. Dr Gabriela worked her way over my whole face, a bit like a sculptor, now and again pausing to assess her creation. Apparently my left side was saggier than my right, so more needles were needed there. Right at the end she told me she was going to give me more definition in my lips and put two small needles in right on the two tips. Afterwards I sat with ice on my face for a while before a lovely soothing mask was applied and I dozed off.

There was a difference as soon as the treatment was finished. I didn't look nearly as bad as I felt I should. My face felt really hot and sore, but actually I didn't look too bad. I looked a bit like I'd been under a sunbed for too long.

'The effects will only get better because not only do the threads provide an immediate lift,' Dr Gabriela told me, 'but they also make the body produce collagen and create collagen threads so the texture of the skin improves over the months following the procedure. Eventually the collagen threads take the place of the PDO threads that gradually vanish.' If you are thinking of having this treatment do make sure you go somewhere that uses the PDO threads because they are the only ones that create collagen in a natural way and do not cause any inflammation. There are plenty of other threads on the market, for example gold ones, but only the PDO will give you the optimum results and are not in any way harmful.

Wrinkle or wrinkle free? Definitely wrinkle free. There was a bit of downtime for me, partly because I do bruise very easily. And for the first few days my whole face felt very tender, as well as red and slightly swollen. Putting on creams was excruciating. The very first evening after the treatment I went out for dinner with a friend and I had to keep telling her not to make me laugh because it hurt. In fact, if you do have this done I would suggest going straight home afterwards, and not straight out on the town like I did. Two days after the treatment I looked worse because the bruises started to appear but they were relatively easy to cover and I carried on as normal, going out and about. I was really pleased with the results early on. My face looked firmer and my skin was glowing. Now, four weeks on, I am absolutely thrilled with it. A friend of mine today asked me if I'd been on holiday. 'You don't look different,' she said. 'Just better.' My lips, incredibly, are more defined. Every time I look at them I remember the two last needles going on and wonder how physically they have translated into my new look lips. 'It's magic,' Dr Gabriela would say if I asked her. I think she may be right.

www.drgabriela.co.uk

Peel away the layers

What I tried: The Mandelic Acid Peel at the michaeljohn Medispa Belgravia

What it does: Takes off the top layer of skin (or more depending on how strong it is).

What I expected: 'Women get addicted to peels,' says my therapist as she wipes an alcohol-soaked swab over my face to prep my skin. I can see why. Although they have a bad reputation for leaving skin red raw, the newest ones are quick, painless, cheaper than lasers and give incredible results. I have a three-minute Mandelic Acid peel. The maximum is eight minutes but that's only if you 'are a smoker or have leathery skin.' Peels basically remove layers of skin to expose new, fresher skin below. The longer they are left on the more layers they remove. There is a slight tingling during and immediately afterwards, which is alleviated by a nourishing post-peel mask. Afterwards my skin is, quite literally, glowing, with a glossiness that looks healthy but almost shiny. I meet a friend for coffee who immediately asks what I've been up to.

What happened: Initially my face feels dry but by the evening though it has calmed down and my skin just looks fabulously polished and utterly squeaky clean. Over the next few days my skin texture improves. There are some bits flaking off, and I have to keep brushing them away, but that only lasts a couple of days. There are some at-home alternatives, which you can read about below.

Home peels have greatly improved in recent years and while they won't give the same results as salon peels or lasers, they will definitely give skin a boost. As promised in the post below I have rounded up some of the better ones out there. Boots No 7 Youthful Glycolic Peel Kit (www.boots.com) is a professionally inspired glycolic peel that gives fast results, while Philosophy Microdelivery Peel Kit (www.johnlewis.com) delivers Vitamin C into the skin during the exfoliation process to brighten and rejuvenate the skin. Dr Dennis Gross Alpha Beta Peel Extra Strength Formula is the only peel on the market that combines five alpha- and beta-hydroxy acids with potent anti-ageing antioxidants. But the easiest to use by far is the DCL Multiaction Penta Peel (michaeljohn.co.uk) — you just take out a peel-soaked pad the size of a cotton pad and wipe it over your face three times a week, leaving it on for five minutes before rinsing. My skin felt incredibly soft after I used it, and looked squeaky clean.

Top Pain and Top Gain

What I tried: The Syneron eMatrixE2

What it does: As we age the collagen levels in the skin deplete, resulting in the appearance of loose, lax skin. But with the Syneron eMatrixE2, this process can be reversed. The machine uses bipolar radio frequency technology to place heat into the lower level of the skin, called the dermis. During the treatment, this heat injures the skin, which elicits a healing response. In other words, the treatment works by damaging the lower dermis of your skin, which in turn makes your skin produce collagen and elastin, thus making it look younger. The big difference with the eMatrixE2 treatment is that the downtime (when you look like a mad woman and can't be seen in public) is dramatically reduced from weeks with a chemical peel or days with a laser to just a few hours depending on how much you do.

What I expected: What most women expect when they undergo a beauty treatment, to be utterly transformed into something resembling my former self. I also know this is not realistic, so, managing expectations, I was hoping for a visible if not dramatic result.

What I experienced: We all know the old saying about suffering to be beautiful. My grandmother would endlessly repeat is as she dragged a comb through my fine, tangled hair. But these days there is a whole new level of suffering. We're talking serious pain. This treatment literally burns your flesh, and you can not only feel it, but smell it. Actually the pain is not that bad at the time, and there are levels of intensity to choose from, so if you're squeamish you can go low. I went as high as possible in order to try for optimum results. My therapist moved a contraption across my face, which beeped as she shot radio frequency rays into my face. She focused on the areas that need it most, the crinkly skin on my eyes and the fine lines underneath them. She went over my face several times. It is not a pleasant experience, it has to be said, but it's not as painful as a chemical peel (apparently) and also much more effective. The bony bits on my face were particularly painful and I did have to focus on the end result to stop myself heading for the door a couple of times. Two weeks after the treatment I went back for a top-up in the form of 'needling', which involved the therapist rolling a roller with hundreds of small needles over my face to reactivate the healing process (and anti-ageing process) started by the eMatrix. After the needling she applied a serum and a mask, which was the nice bit. I was then given the torture instrument and instructed to use it as and when needed, after a bad night's sleep for example, or when I am looking particularly jowly.

What happened afterwards: On the way home from the eMatrix treatment my eyes started stinging, and my skin felt like it was on fire. This heat is apparently a good sign, it means the treatment has worked and the lower dermis is healing. By the time I got home I could barely open my eyes and I did wonder whether I had finally gone over the top. Would I be blinded by my own vanity? I called the therapist who told me this is an unusual side effect and that it would pass. Before I went to sleep I managed a look in the mirror. I looked like the victim of a brutal mugging, with swollen bits under my eyes and red patches all over. I decided the only thing for it was to try for some beauty sleep....

The next morning I could see, and the swelling had started to go down, but I was still in no state to go anywhere and my face still felt like it was being cooked. My husband kept looking at me and shaking his head. I kept moisturising and soothing my skin and by that evening, I had definitely turned a corner. The following days the results started to literally shine through. It was as if my skin had been glossed with a dewy finish — it just glowed. It was luminous from the moment I woke up to the moment I went to bed. For the first time in years I went out without wearing any make-up and no one asked me if I was ill. I looked like I had just come from a facial all the time; fresh and healthy. The results kept getting better every day, and once another week had passed I did the needling treatment on my own. I was probably not as ruthless as my therapist (few people are, but she gets the results), but I think I did all right, and I am getting braver every time. I will definitely go back for another eMatrix treatment, I have never experienced anything as effective this. Rebecca says three should be enough, and then I just need to keep up with the needling. No pain, no gain.

Wrinkles or Wrinkle Free? Definitely wrinkle free, but be prepared for the immediate after effects being uncomfortable.

Star Skin Product

What? Dior Capture Total Dream Skin

Why? Every time I use it I think about Sharon Stone and how it is possible to look incredibly sexy after 50. Added to which, this has a texture that makes you feel good about your skin. It seems to smooth away uneven skin tone or surface imperfections.

Top Tip

Take your make-up off as soon as you get home instead of

leaving it until you're too tired to do a good job.

Star Cleansing Product

What? Eve Lom Cleanser

Why? This is one of those cult beauty products that anyone who knows anything about the beauty industry will invariably put on a top ten list. I hadn't heard of it until a friend very kindly gave me a pot and now I'm hooked. It has been around for 25 years and was developed by Eve herself using herbs from her grandmother's garden in the Czech Republic. Eve has since sold the company to SpaceNK but the cleanser remains the same magical, rich cleanser that she created all those years ago. There is a massage routine with it (Eve doesn't really believe in creams, she believes in stimulating the skin through touch) and the few times I have had time to do this I have seen a difference. But usually I just cleanse and luxuriate…

Star serum

What? Dr. Viel's X118 Intense Hydrating Serum
Why? This is one of those comforting products I can no longer imagine being without. It glides on like silk, leaving your skin feeling super nourished and hydrated. It is especially effective when you've had any kind of treatment such as a peel as it really calms and soothes the skin. If I ever become a multi-millionaire I am going to buy it in bulk and out it all over my body, especially my hands.

Top Tip

Around three times a week I use a face mask. I mix them up a bit so go for an exfoliating mask, followed by a hydrating one and maybe a soothing one or a mask stuffed full of active ingredients. My favourites at the moment include the Sisley Rose, the Clarins HydraQuench Cream Mask and Dr Gabriela Harley Street Clinic Advanced Molecular Mask. And you don't always have to take time out to put on a mask. I usually pop one on after I've cleansed in the morning and then potter around getting ready for the day while it does its work. Obviously if it's one like Dr Gabriela's that is infused in paper then you need to lie down. But whatever you do, use a mask every other day to keep the wrinkles away.

5

It's only skin deep...

'I spit into the face of time that has transfigured me.'
W.B. Yeats

I hadn't really thought about natural skincare until one product changed my life. In fact, I had vaguely thought about it, but I just assumed it could not be as effective as products that were specifically created to hydrate my skin or make it look younger. Then I interviewed a woman called Geraldine Howard who is the founder of a company called Aromatherapy Associates, a company that sells its natural skin care range in over 50 countries. She told me all about how she was a firm believer in using natural products and especially rose oil, and sent me a sample of her Aromatherapy Associates Renewing Rose Massage & Body Oil. 'This is my desert island product,' she told me.

Geraldine studied under the legendary aromatherapist Micheline Arcier. 'I had always been concerned about the harmful effects of synthetic cosmetics,' she says. 'And then I met Micheline who was in her sixties and who had the most radiant skin ever and so few lines. From that day on I never used anything else.' As soon as the rose oil arrived I tried it. I put it on my legs and arms. It went on smoothly and my skin felt hydrated. It also smelt nice. And there was one rather more significant effect.

For about two years I had been suffering from eczema around my ankles and on the sides of my knees. Up until then I had led a blissfully eczema-free existence. I don't know what caused it, my doctor thought it might be stress and prescribed a cream that alleviated the itching a little. But as anyone who has ever suffered from eczema knows it is the most pernicious irritating thing. And not only for the person who has it. 'Stop itching,' my husband would yell as I tried to contain the urge to scratch at my ankles until they were raw and bleeding.

After one application of the miracle rose oil, I stopped itching. With almost immediate effect. It was the most incredible thing I had ever experienced with a product, and it changed my view on the whole natural/organic versus non-organic debate.

Having now spent a long time researching anti-ageing products and their effectiveness, I am more impressed by the natural ones than I was, but I am not prepared to limit myself to them. The downside to synthetic creams of course is the potentially harmful ingredients they contain. The skin is our largest organ, and there are studies to suggest it absorbs 80 per cent of what we put on it. So if we use creams with toxins, it absorbs those toxins.

So what to do? I turn for advice to an expert, Ingeborg van Lotringen, Beauty Director of *Cosmopolitan Magazine* in London. Ingeborg looks like a prettier, younger Claudia Schiffer. She is the kind of woman who, the minute you meet her, makes you think 'I must make more of an effort'.

The list of possible dangers makes for scary reading. Silicone, for example, that is often used in creams coats your skin and can impede its breathing. Mineral oils also tend to block the skin. Parabens that are often widely used as preservatives in cosmetics have been linked to hormonal imbalances. Synthetic fragrances often contain harmful chemicals.

'As far as I'm concerned, organic versus non-organic is a moot point unless you're of the persuasion that everything you eat and do should be organic in some way — and if you don't care very much about the effectiveness of your products,' she tells me. Ingeborg argues that rather than look at organic versus non-organic we should look for 'clean' skincare. 'This is a far more realistic and achievable way to select your products, and their rise was driven by the original surge of organic and 'natural' skincare.' By clean Ingeborg means products that are free of non-essential but cheap (and sometimes potentially dangerous) additives like colourants, synthetic fragrance, harsh sulphates, phtalates and some parabens.

'This trend (brands like Ren and Liz Earle are good examples) has really changed the skincare market for the better, with loads of affordable brands now following the same principles. So if you're worried about what you're putting on your skin (whether or not any of these very regulated ingredients really do any harm is not yet proven), it's easy to cut out the most contested ingredients. Formulating 100 per cent organic products is extremely difficult and limits you to just a few textures and product types. Millions has been pumped into research of natural active ingredients and there are great brands out there (l'Occitane, Decléor, Origins) that are mainly "natural" and "clean" but also employ the latest delivery system technologies to make sure their actives actually penetrate the skin. They see no point in limiting themselves to being 100 per cent organic and neither do I.'

One example of this is Jurlique Rosewater Balancing Mist. It is now on my 'can't live without' list. It's a delicate mist made with essential rose oil, which is between a toner and a moisturiser, and preps the face perfectly for your daily hydrating cream. Jurlique says they 'apply advanced technologies to biodynamic ingredients from our Australian farm to create high performance, potent skin care.'

I think what always used to worry me about organic ranges is do they actually do anything? And if they are so effective, then how can brands like Chanel and La Prairie go on charging such huge amounts of money for creams that are anything but natural?

According to Dr Mohammed Amir, Specialist Dermatologist at the Aesthetic Clinic in Abu Dhabi, organic products are unproven. 'All these natural things can hydrate,' he says, 'but nothing more. There is no research to back them up.' But he concedes that while giant companies such as Chanel and La Prairie do have research to back their products up, there are questions about how effective these creams can be, given that they have to be suitable for the mass market.

'They can't be too strong because it would reflect very badly if people had an adverse reaction to them,' he says. 'For really effective anti-ageing you need medical products that are prescribed for your skin.'

I have to say I have loved using pricey creams like Chanel and La Prairie when I've had the chance. Just the packaging makes you feel great. And the stuff feels wonderful. I particularly found the La Prairie Cellular Swiss cream and oil a great combination. Although I would have to admit there was not a massive difference in my skin compared to when I was using a cheaper brand.

The rather tackily named Jeunesse Global is one company that is combining cosmetics with science. Their premise is based on stem cell technology and their products are high in growth factors. According to a spokesman for the company the serum, for example, contains over 200 key human growth factors and cellular messengers all of which help your skin to rejuvenate. I have listened to interviews with their main scientist, Dr Nathan Newman, and he sounds credible. Although I had the impression he was more taken with the actual stem cell work (ie injecting body fat back into patients in the same way the Italian Nip and Tuck team do) than the creams.

I did wonder in fact if the creams were just a way to make money to fund the research he wants to do. If Simon Erani, a dermatologist with the Somme Institute is to be believed, then that is probably the most useful thing creams will do.

'Essentially cosmetic companies are great marketing companies,' he says, 'and that's all. If it really worked, they wouldn't change it. They would stop coming up with new creams every year. Basically they're just creating new ways to get you to part with your money.'

The Somme Institute has developed a range of skincare products using a formula they call MDT5, based on molecular dispersion technology. In simple terms it effectively dispersed vitamins and proteins to go deep into the skin to repair damage.

'Next time a cream tells you on the box it is a clinical breakthrough, ask for the evidence,' says Simon. 'We have evidence that our product works, that it penetrates the skin and that it creates great results.' Simon tells me that in the course of researching other creams they tested everything from Crème de la Mer to Chanel to the low-end brands. 'Some were good moisturisers and some plumped up the skin for a few hours, but that's about it,' he says.

The fact that the world is going increasingly organic and natural is proven by the fact that the natural and organic skincare market is now worth around $8 billion globally. As demand has increased, the skincare industry has undergone a revolution in order to meet that demand.

When I wrote my last book about anti-ageing in 2008 the watchword was active ingredients; ingredients that actually have an effect on your skin, that are able to change its texture or tone. It still is, but nowadays those active ingredients are natural, for example orange peel, olive oil, royal jelly and pomegranate. And not only do they improve your skin, they won't do you any harm while doing so. But will they actually do you any good?

Yes they will according to Geraldine Howard. 'I don't know anyone that wouldn't benefit from some rose oil,' she says. 'And actually a lot of modern cosmetics are derived from natural ingredients. Hyaloronic acid for example occurs naturally in the body. Of course it can be made synthetically but I prefer the natural option, it just feels safer. As far as I'm concerned, the only place you really need synthetics is in hair care. You need silicones to coat the hair and to make it shine in hair conditioners.'

I am going to follow Ingeborg's lead and use a combination of products. I am loving the natural oils from Aromatherapy Associates, everything from the Fine Line Oil to the Rose Face Oil to rose body oil. As well as the products from ila-spa (see the details section below). But at the same time I am also drawn to products that are slightly more scientific. I have always found the SkinCeuticals range effective, as well as Philosophy. So I start with a synthetic serum, then put on the organic oil, then a synthetic moisturiser, followed of course by sunblock. I am moving away though from the purely cosmetic brands such as Chanel for my skin care. I think the combination of organic and medical might just be the happy medium I'm after.

The cleavage booster treatment

Apparently we Brits are blessed with the biggest breasts in Europe. The average breast size in the UK is between 36C and 34E, and it is increasing every year. Ten years ago it was 34B.So how do we best look after these prized assets? And especially at this time of year when we are busy showing our curves off in skimpy cocktail dresses.

Well one thing is a revolutionary treatment that promises to bring out the best in your breasts without resorting to scalpels or needles.

Probably like many women I didn't really bother about my breasts until five or six years ago when it occurred to me that it was a bit weird to moisturise arms, torso, legs and tummy and yet avoid the breasts and started rubbing it with moisturiser like I did the rest of my body. If I'm feeling particularly rich I sometimes invest in some bust cream or other, and I do now religiously protect my décolletage from the sun. But while I'm a sucker for a salon, it has never occurred to me to go for a treatment specifically targetting my embonpoint.

Called the Cellcosmet Swiss Bust Contour Defining Treatment, this therapy is designed to reshape and tone the décolleté and bust. Anything with the word Swiss in it gives me faith. There's something bracing, and no-nonsense about it. And they really do know their stuff when it comes to anti-ageing — after all those rich ladies flocking to spas on Lake Geneva could go anywhere in the world to hold back time. But they opt for Swiss expertise. So I arrived at the Aldo Coppola salon on Sloane Avenue in an optimistic mood.

My therapist, a sensible-looking lady called Sharon, lead me downstairs to the treatment room where she instructed me to take off my shirt, bra and necklace. She then gave me a towel to cover my breasts, which I thought was sweet, if a bit unnecessary seeing as she was going to spend the next hour doing much more than just looking at them.

Before we began, Sharon explained to me how essential it is to take good care of your breasts because there are no muscles there do the job of maintaining them for you. Your breasts are supported by a kind of natural bra of connective tissue that goes from underneath the chest to the neck so making sure this skin is in as good a shape as possible is essential. "The sagging begins from the back of the neck," she explained. "So don't forget to bring your cream all the way back there when you apply it."

The treatment started with a gentle exfoliation where Sharon rubbed my breasts with a grainy scrub designed to take off dead skin and prepare the breasts for the treatment ahead. The skin around the breast area is very sensitive, and I thought this might be painful, but it wasn't at all. I regularly exfoliate my face, legs, arms and stomach it has never dawned on me that my boobs could benefit from a bit of exfoliation too.

The bust is not an area one is used to having treated or massaged, at least I'm not. Funnily enough it didn't seem strange or uncomfortable in any way, which I had been expecting.

After the exfoliation she put a hot wet towel on them to remove any excess product but, she explained, she was careful to leave some grains there for the massage process "because the breast area is never exfoliated, so it needs to be done more than once". After the hot towel Sharon sprayed some sort of scented water on my breasts, which certainly woke me (and them) up a bit. The massage oil was next, a mixture of rosehip, borage, evening primrose, carrot, and geranium essential oil.

After the oil it was time for the mask, which contains a marine algae complex to help slow down the loss of collagen and elastin, (the two most important ingredients in keeping your cleavage pert) spirulina, amino acids, flavinoids and other nutrients that are good for cell regeneration and tissue repair, along with dry witch hazel extract and carrot essential oil to soften the skin. Before it is applied Sharon mixes a concentrate into it that includes kigeline extract, which has an anti-slackening, contouring effect whilst improving skin's elasticity and lilac floral water, which has toning, astringent, regenerating and softening properties.

This is what you might call a 'smart mask'. Not only does it do all of the above, but it mimics your natural skin functions and is thus able to restructure the dermis. This is what is so groundbreaking about this treatment. It uses cellular and plant technology, taking into account your hormonal identity and physiological age. This method of cell therapy is based on the same method that is used in medicine when a sick organ is treated or stimulated by young cellular tissue coming from a similar organ.

So in effect the cell extracts in the mask communicate with your skin's cells, and basically tell them to regenerate. This does sound a little sci-fi but as it's a Swiss brand I'm inclined to believe it. I just can't imagine a Swiss person lying.

Incorporating a trademarked CellControl™ Method, the products utilise up to 98% of the cells' natural activity compared to the average 3-5% of other so-called cellular ranges, helping to regenerate, rejuvenate and re-energise the skin faster and more efficiently.

The mask was left on for half an hour or so to dry into a greenish rubbery mass.

The treatment, which arrived in the UK two and a half years ago, has been going for 30 years in Switzerland. According to Sharon ladies of all ages are doing the treatment. "Hormonal variations throughout adolescence, pregnancy and menopause can all result in changes in the breasts," she says. "Alongside this, fluctuations in weight, an ill-fitting bra, not having the correct support during exercise and abuse in the sun can cause a slackening of the breast, which the treatment can help to improve."

Sharon peeled the mask off and it came off in pretty much one go rather like a sheet of thick greeny-grey blancmange. Instantly my skin looks glowing and hydrated, as well as smooth and extremely clean. I slightly feel like I've been neglecting it all this time and it is glowing after its first forty-five minutes of attention ever.

I tell Sharon how pleased I am but add that surely this effect won't last. She disagrees. Sharon has had the treatment herself and utterly swears by it. "I saw a huge improvement," she told me. "My breasts are much firmer and have even lifted." She has had it four times so far and recommends that for any dramatic result you should go for a course of five treatments, four times a year, and then top-up treatments now and again. But she says that after just one treatment the bust is left looking smoother and more rounded. I would agree with that. I could definitely see a difference afterwards, especially on my décolletage; the skin texture was much better and even seemed slightly less sun damaged than before.

According to Sharon the effects can last for two to three months, especially if you adopt their homecare routine too. They make a "revitalizing cellular bust cream-gel" that is an extension of the actual treatment in that it contains the same cell technology.

I have been using mine and really like it; it's a thick substance, slightly reminiscent of a caramel sauce in colour and texture, which you rub around and on your breasts and up to the back of your neck on a daily basis, ideally twice daily. There are some products that just really feel like they're doing some good, and this is one of them. I have been using it now for a week and the effect has been two-fold. My skin looks clearer and is in much better condition than before. And my bust really does look firmer. It could just have perked up as a result of all the attention it's getting, but whatever it is, it's working. And I'll be looking for a low-cut dress for this year's Christmas party.

www.aldocoppola.co.uk
www.cellcosmet.co.uk

Star Product

What? Aromatherapy Associates Renewing Rose Massage & Body Oil

Why? I don't know where to begin. This is one of the best products I have ever come across and now that I've found it I never want to be without it again. Geraldine Howard, the founder of Aromatherapy Associates, calls it her 'desert island product' and I can see why. After using in ONCE the eczema around my ankles and on my knees was cured. Unbelievable. Added to which, it is the best, most comforting and effective body moisturiser I have ever used.

Seriously Serum

Serum... it's one of those words, a bit like anti-oxidant or peptide, that sends me into a panic. I know I should be using one, but what is it, and what does it do?

According to my sources, serums are the latest thing in anti-ageing and we should all be using them daily. The reason being that they contain active ingredients and are chemically formulated with smaller molecules so that they can penetrate deeper into the skin than your moisturiser.

Needless to say there are hundreds of serums on the market but I have tried a selection for you.

The first one I tried is the best value, the Olay Regenerist Microsculpting Serum. I like Olay products. My mother, a million years ago, used to use Oil of Ulay, and she is a woman who has a rather bare bathroom — unlike me of course who can hardly move for the bottles and jars of unguents and miracle workers. If it was good enough for my mum it's good enough for me, and the glittery fluid does slide on rather smoothly. I like the texture and feel of it; my skin feels quenched after use. Another good bargain is from No 7: the Protect and Perfect Advanced Serum. There is a less rich one for younger skin, but I like the advanced range, and this glides on nicely.

The big advantage with serums as I said is the active ingredients. These are things like Vitamin C and anti-oxidants (such as green tea) that actually have an effect on your skin. The disadvantage with the most powerful of them, Vitamin C, is that just in the same way that your body can't store it, it loses its efficiency once the bottle is opened. So beware of products purporting to contain Vitamin C.

The Estée Lauder Midnight Recovery comes in a brown bottle to protect the active ingredients inside. It is not a cheap option but can last up to six months and is excellent for nourishing your tired skin overnight. A very elegant Parisian friend of mine says she has been using it for years and swears by it. I have to believe her because her glowing skin cannot be down to her healthy lifestyle — she does nothing but smoke and drink coffee.

Another way to protect the ingredients in serums is to put the product into small vials that you open one at a time. This is the case with Eucerin Hyaluron-Filler Concentrate, a serum that plumps up your wrinkles with hyaluronic acid and glycine saponin — no you don't need to know what they are. Again this is a smooth formula that makes your skin feel enriched, even if you are poorer. Dermalogica also does this with its Multivitamin capsule, another one of my favourites.

Don't be scared by serums, just treat them with care.

Star Product

What? La Praire Cellular Swiss Ice Crystal Cream and Ice Crystal Dry Oil

Why? Just using these products make you feel like a millionaire. OK so you probably have to be a millionaire to be able to afford them but I have to say if you possibly can do it, they are actually quite good value for money. Not only are they effective — I really did notice a difference in my skin tone and texture after using them for a few weeks — but they last a lot longer than cheaper products. So they may be four times the price, but they last four times longer, at least. And you feel like a film star just picking the tub up.

Beyond Organic

What I tried: an ila-spa treatment

What I experienced: While most people probably dread going to the office on a Monday morning, for the 27 or so workers at the ila-spa offices close to Woodstock in the Cotswolds it's a chance to meditate. On Monday mornings, Carly, the head of the spa division, leads the meditation session to put the staff in the right frame of mind to create products that are, as Denise Leicester the founder describes them, 'beyond organic'.

What Denise means by beyond organic is that the products

used to make ila-spa are not just organically grown. 'We also guarantee that our products are extremely pure, 'says Denise, an attractive woman with thick glossy brown hair and an open, kind face who founded ila-spa in 2005. 'Not only in where they have come from, but how they have been handled. I believe the way things are made is very important. It's a little bit like cooking, there needs to be a lovely energy around the process.'

There is certainly plenty of that at ila HQ. The place feels more like a luxury spa than the seat of a thriving company that sells its products all over the world.

The first thing you notice when you walk into reception is how good it smells. That is down to their jasmine and sandalwood incense sticks, as well as room diffusers. The next thing you notice is how NICE everyone is. It's almost like you have to be a certain type of person to work there. I can't imagine any of the ten or so staff I meet having a bad word to say about anyone. The environment is the opposite of toxic.

A trained aromatherapist, Denise started creating her own cosmetics when she developed ME and started having terrible reactions to shop-bought products. 'The final straw was when I was on a flight back from a holiday in France with my husband and I bought some serum. I dabbed some around my eyes and by the time we landed my eyes were swollen and red and I had started to develop blisters. I also noticed some products would leave me feeling terribly drained.'

Denise spent a year travelling the globe to source the purest and highest quality raw materials, from rose petals in India to Argan Oil in Morocco. 'I wanted to use sources that help the local community,' explains Denise. 'So for example in Morocco the ladies who work for the Argan oil cooperatives can shell the kernels in their own homes so they don't have to leave their children. We use producers who have a respect for nature and we want to take our produce beyond just a certificate saying its organic. We want to make a successful beautiful luxury product that benefits the local community. It is possible to do both.'

One of the great success stories for ila has been its collaboration with the Kayapó tribe in the Amazonian rain forest. Denise first heard about the tribe during a talk in London.

'The conclusion was that the only way to save the rain forest is through developing the economies of the indigenous people. I immediately wanted to know how ila could help to do this and so we started to buy their Babassu oil, a wonderfully light oil that comes from the seeds of the Babassu palm.'

For the Kayapó tribe the skin is sacred, it is their spirit so they are experts at caring for it. They also have an enormous respect for nature. 'Rain forest people will never kill anything,' says Denise. 'They take the leaves or the berries but they make sure nothing is damaged.'

The oil the Kayapó produce goes into the ila-spa Rainforest Range, a highly restorative and renewing range. Denise is thrilled with the cooperation and keen to visit the tribe. 'It's a three week trip there though and a three-week trip back so it's hard to find the time.'

I ask her how effective all these products actually are. 'Anything that is wild and not farmed is a lot more vibrant and more potent and has more energy,' she says. 'Obviously if you go down the natural route it's going to take a little longer to get results. And if what you want is no wrinkles at all then you're going to have to use chemicals. But if you want radiance and hydration this can definitely be achieved through an organic range. We are also developing more potent products now using the plant's stem cells. Take the rose for example, within the stalk is a series of mother cells that hold all the information about the plant. These can be extracted without damaging the plant. We are working on a range with a German pharmacist to create a plant-based cosmeceutical range and getting really great results.'

Denise believes that the benefits of using a holistic, organically sourced and prepared product will have an effect on more than just your skin. 'The name ila is Sanskrit and means mother earth, flow and integrity. I noticed that when I used products made with chemicals I would feel emotionally out of sorts. The beauty of using something vibrant and organic is that you feel grounded, and your energy levels rise too.'

Legally you can make a cream with only 70 per cent natural ingredients and call it 'natural'. Denise thinks consumers are becoming more and more wary of products that contain damaging ingredients such as parabens.

'Much in the same was as people are questioning what they eat, they are questioning what they put on their skin,' she says. 'We all know now that anything we put on our skin is absorbed. If you said to people 'I'm going to put a lot of poison on my skin but I think it's going to make me look good' they'd think you were mad.'

'The choice of what you use really comes down to the question of what beauty is to you. What is being beautiful? If it is harmony and balance both inside and outside then you should switch to a product that puts you back in touch with yourself and with nature, a product that uses a vibrant ingredient that is part of the earth.'

To a lot of you this will sound like new-age chat. And I must admit when I first came across ila, I wondered if it was veering that way. One of the first things Denise talked to me about was the importance of getting the right Vaastu for the business. I looked at her and thought 'oh help', but actually she has such a grounded, intelligent manner that it's impossible to think she's cranky. I didn't know what Vaastu was, and for those of you who are interested, it's the Hindu (and in some cases Buddhist) equivalent of Feng Shui.

I am now a convert. OK maybe not to the idea of Vasstu, but to ila products. Denise said I would need to wait for results but my skin looked radiant and refreshed the very first time I used their serum and face oil. Their bath salts and body products are incredible as well.

A Lift too far

What I tried: Le Lift de Chanel anti-wrinkle and firming cream

Fantasy: That my face would be instantly lifted and I would look as beautiful as the packaging the product comes in. They claim that the cream contains an exclusive natural ingredient called 3.5 DA, which has the ability to sense what your skin needs and also boost the production of youth proteins that make your skin more supple and elastic.

Reality: You can't ever be disappointed with anything from Chanel. Just the sight of the little black box is enough to make you want to whoop for joy. But the reality of this (however gorgeous) product is that it really doesn't lift your face. It plumps it and it is an excellent moisturiser, but for a real lift you need more drastic measures.

Star Product

What? Jurlique Rosewater Balancing Mist

Why? Another 'can't live without' product that I use all day every day either to freshen up my skin or to hydrate it or just to pep myself up. This delicate mist made with essential rose oil is something between a toner and a moisturiser, and preps the face perfectly for your daily hydrating cream.

6

Staying young in the sun

'A woman has the age she deserves.'
Coco Chanel

We have all seen them. Those women who look like a cross between Brigitte Bardot and one of her donkeys. Or one of your favourite leather handbags. Your first thought when you spot one is; 'that is a woman who has had too much sun'. Your second thought is; 'how can I avoid ending up like that?'

On a wonderful holiday in the south of France last year, my husband and I rented a convertible Citroën so we could explore the Riviera's winding cliff-top roads in style.

Of course that sounds impossibly glamorous, but it wasn't. I spent the entire time either shielding my face with my hands or clutching a large straw hat around it to protect my skin from the sun.

I am the opposite of a sun-worshipper: I am a dedicated sun-avoider. I can't bear to be exposed to direct sunlight because I know the terrible damage it will do to my complexion.

So hiring a convertible car was a very bad idea as far as I was concerned, but I had bowed to pressure from my husband and our three excited children.

We returned from France to a gloriously sunny England, where a friend who came to meet me at Gatwick Airport suggested we go for a drink.

'I know a lovely pub where we can sit outside,' she said.

A mild panic immediately took hold. It was 3pm: I had last put on sunscreen at 9am. All those hours later my sunscreen needed reapplying to be effective, but it was buried deep in my suitcase in the boot of my friend's car, and I didn't want to make a fuss.

As we settled at a table in direct sunlight — the only one available — all I could think about was grabbing my friend's car keys and finishing my gin and tonic in the shade of her passenger seat.

I admonished myself for not wearing a hat, feeling the strong afternoon rays burning my skin despite my attempt to shield my face with my hands. The more she enthused about this rare glimpse of sun, the less I felt I could suggest we move inside — especially as she had just driven miles to meet me.

I wasn't always like this. Growing up in England in the Seventies, it was a crime to stay indoors if the sun was shining. As a teenager I lay on a beach covered in oil, which accelerated tanning rather than protecting my skin.

But then I grew up and I travelled the world talking to experts about how to avoid wrinkles. The message was the same from London to Lusaka, from Geneva to Jamaica: avoid the sun.

So, since then, that is what I have done — even if it means rearranging a complex seating plan to sit in the shade, as I once did when I visited a friend for lunch. I ended up sitting next to the most boring person at the table — possibly on the planet — but at least I didn't age during the starter. Even if I did at a few points during it lose the will to live at all.

My husband's theory is that rather than avoiding the sun I am avoiding our children as they splash about in a pool. I am happy to look after the children, in the shade. But it's not like I miss out on things I would otherwise be doing. I hate getting my hair wet so would avoid the pool anyway. And if everyone wants to sit in the sun for a cup of tea I either wear a hat or engineer a bit of shade. contrary to popular belief, you can actually tan in the shade. You just don't burn.

Sometimes of course there is no avoiding the sun. I went to my son's sports day last weekend and it was the most glorious day. The picnic was in the middle of a field, with not a jot of shade around. But there was no way I was going to skulk into the surrounding woods and miss out on the chilled wine for spectators, so I doubled up on the sun screen, popped on a floppy hat and went for it.

Skin cancer accounts for around four per cent of all cancers in the UK. The fastest-growing group is the over-65s: skin cancer diagnosis among them has risen by five times over the last 30 years, due mainly to sun exposure during holidays abroad.

Aside from the risk of cancer, nothing ages us like the sun. We can spend our life savings on creams like La Prairie or Crème de la Mer, but they won't make a jot of difference if we expose ourselves to the sun's rays. Whatever is happening I apply sunscreen every single day, whether I'm in southern Spain or Scotland.

I'm in good company. Supermodel Elle McPherson has said: 'Every morning I brush my teeth and put my sunscreen on.'

The first rigorous study of its kind, conducted in Australia, has shown that year-round use of sunscreen significantly slows skin ageing caused by the sun's ultraviolet rays.

Researchers discovered that adults who regularly use broad-spectrum sunscreen — which protects against ultraviolet A (UVA) and B rays (UVB) — age less quickly.

The difference between UVA and UVB rays is that UVA rays exist even when the sun doesn't shine. They are stronger than UVB rays so can penetrate the skin more deeply. They also permeate glass and some clothing, hence the need to wear sunscreen every day. If it's light outside, you're being zapped by rays.

UVB rays are the ones that cause sunburn. They are stronger in the summer and also more usually responsible for skin cancers, although UVA rays also contribute to cancer.

Received wisdom used to be that UVA rays — the rays emitted by tanning beds — weren't harmful. Now, of course, nobody with any sense would use a tanning bed given how dangerous they are. Studies show that using them before the age of 30 can increase the risk of skin cancer by up to 75 per cent.

In some research published a couple of years ago in Australia's Annals of Internal Medicine 903 people, aged between 25 and 55, were randomly assigned to two groups. One group was asked to apply sunscreen with a sun protection factor (SPF) of 15+ to their head, neck, arms and hands each morning and after bathing, spending time in the sun or sweating. The other group was told to apply sunscreen at their own discretion.

The backs of their hands were examined for microscopic changes in skin ageing at the beginning of the study, then four-and-a-half years later.

The results show that adults who regularly used sunscreen were less likely to develop wrinkles than adults who didn't.

'But we live in England, not Australia,' I hear you chant. 'The sun never shines here.'

Don't believe it for a moment.

Skincare and anti-ageing specialist Tina Richards explains: 'I put on sunscreen before I even open the curtains — and I live in Wimbledon!'

So what actually happens to your skin when it's exposed to the sun?

Tina says: 'If the skin's unprotected, UVA rays enter your skin and travel down into the deep dermis to the collagen and elastin in less than a minute.'

Collagen and elastin work together to stop the skin sagging and ageing, hence the need to protect them. When unprotected skin is exposed to the sun even for a very short period of time, damaged molecules start attacking healthy ones.

The good news is that you can keep your skin sun-safe with the right precautions. Forget expensive lotions and potions: the single most crucial weapon is to use sunscreen with an SPF of at least 15 every day, even when it's raining.

You need to think of the sun as your enemy. A ferocious monster to be fought on all levels. Your weapons include first and foremost sun cream. For my face I use Clinique City Block Sun Protection Factor 25. Then I use a moisturising cream by Dermalogica with an SPF of 15. On top of that I use Laura Mercier Mineral Make-up powder, which also carries an SPF of 15. All this I use on my face, neck and décolletage. Always making sure I brush and smooth upwards on my neck. Plaster on as many layers of protective creams and make-up as you can, there is no shame in overdoing it.

In my handbag I carry Bioderma sun cream for the face, décolletage and hand. It carries a SPF of 50. I use it on the backs of my hands throughout the day to protect them. For my body I use a cheaper brand, maybe Nivea or something similar, which I put onto any part of my body that is exposed to the sun.

Put sunscreen on in the morning after your moisturiser, and

keep it in your handbag for reapplication during the day. If you're outside in the sun, reapply sunscreen every four hours or so, and don't forget to put it on the backs of your hands too.

'Don't even go out to hang the washing up without protecting your skin,' adds Tina Richards. 'If you go for a walk in the sun wear a large hat and don't ever lie in the sun, you can get tanned in the shade as well.'

My 15-year-old daughter Olivia calls me 'Sunscreen Sunscream' but I don't mind. What matters is that my children inherit good habits and stay safe — and I'll do whatever it takes to achieve that. Even if I am labelled a sunscreen bore.

Don't forget your décolletage

Dr Marian Coutinho, a dermatologist at the Kaya skin Clinic in Abu Dhabi, says another thing we must do is look after our necks and décolletage. 'When you are applying sun screens and moisturizers bring them all the way down to your neck and décolletage area,' she says. I have started to wear a silk scarf (something French women do very well) in order to protect my décolletage. I see a lot of women with bad sun damage to their cleavages. Beware of making this mistake. A great friend of mine has a completely red chest. And it is the result of getting very badly burned once in the Swiss Alps, during the WINTER. She was having a long lunch with friends and hadn't put any sunscreen on at all. After lunch she looked at herself in the mirror and her chest was covered in blisters. That was five years ago and it still has a red hue.

The avoiding sun-damage skincare routine

Every day you should cleanse, tone and moisturise before you put on your sunscreen. If you are under 35 then use eye gel, if you're older use an eye cream. Every night use a night cream with an active ingredient like Vitamin C or green tea. If you are over 25 then use a serum as well.

Dr Naina Sachdev, a Berverly Hills based dermatologist who is more well-known as 'Dr Naina', sums up. 'Just do the same on the outside as you do on the inside,' she says. 'Use creams with green tea, for example, or amino peptides that promote cell to cell regeneration like the Olay Regenerist Precision range. When you buy a cream look at the list of ingredients, look for green tea, vitamin E or Hyaluronic acids. Ask the sales assistant "does my cream have pentapeptides in it?'" "Does it have antioxidants in it?'"

She also suggests that you exfoliate once a week and use a moisturising mask. These are both things you can do at home. She suggests a non-abrasive exfoliator like the Dermalogica Daily Microfoliant. If you can, you should have a facial and a microdermabrasion every month. The latter is a treatment that removes dead skin cells and basically vacuums them up, leaving your complexion clean and fresh. 'One of the most ageing things for your skin is leaving dead cells on it,' says Dr Naina, 'so it is essential to cleanse thoroughly and use regular treatments.'

Tina Richards says the most important part of your care regime is the home care you give to your skin every day. 'This is where it really adds up,' she says. 'You can really make a difference to the way your skin looks.'

Dr Marian Coutinho says that dermatologically speaking there are three levels of age control and that we need to work on all three to get the best results. First there is the outer level as mentioned above. Another treatment Dr Coutinho recommends is glycolic peels. 'I would not suggest a chemical peel for all skins,' she says, 'but glycolic peels are made with fruit acid obtained from sugar cane so not as harsh. However, if you have one you will have to avoid the sun for a few days afterwards.'

Peel or no peel, she suggests we should all stay out of the sun completely between 11 and 4pm.

In order to treat the next level, the dermis and the collagen, she suggests various laser-based treatments like photo-facials or the fraxel laser. 'These treatments heat up the skin and help stimulate the fibroblast cells that make collagen and increased collagen production will improve the appearance of small lines and wrinkles as well as open pores.'

The final layer is muscular layer. For this one option is pads that transmit micro currents that stimulate your muscles. 'This makes the muscles on the face and neck tighter and firms up the jaw line,' says Dr Coutinho. 'In this category I also put Botox but I would say it is not a permanent solution, you need to do the other things as well.'

There is, thankfully, a cheaper and more natural alternative to these expensive therapies; facial exercises. You just exercise your facial muscles like you do your bodily ones. One of the leading experts in this field is Carolyn Cleaves who is based in the US. 'Facial exercises are one of the fastest growing fitness programs happening today. Not only can you rid yourself of wrinkles exercising the facial muscles, you can also redefine the cheekbones and jaw line, as well as the nose,' she says. 'Facial exercises help alleviate the papery skin around the neck and under the eyes. Dark circles fade away along with that tired look. The lips become fuller and the nose becomes more defined. In other words, you regain that youthful, dynamic look you had when you were young. And, it's all natural.' carolynsfacialfit-ness.com.

Diet as a weapon against the sun

Drinking a mug of green tea 30 minutes before exposing yourself to the sun's rays is a bit like putting on sunscreen on the inside. Similarly with vitamin C, which you should take half an hour before you go in the sun. It will give some resistance, but doesn't last long.

'When we go out in the sun our levels of the co-enzyme Q10, vitamin E and other anti-oxidants decrease by 50% in ten minutes,' says Dr Naina. 'So it makes sense to increase anti-oxidants before sun exposure. Prepare your body half an hour before sun exposure. Put on the sunscreen of course, but also drink a cup of decaffeinated green tea.'

Dr Naina suggests that if you are in a warm climate you should begin each day with an anti-oxidant loaded breakfast starting with a mixed fruit juice.

'Each fruit has different anti-oxidants so why deprive yourself by sticking to just one?' she says. 'Mix them up and benefit from as many as you can.'

Following the juice you could have some egg whites, rice cakes, some walnuts. These are all foods that will not create or feed any food intolerances (which are inflammatory and therefore ageing) but are high in protein or antioxidants. You could add some red grapes, which are rich in the anti-oxidant resveratrol.

'You should also drink a lot of water throughout the day,' adds Dr Naina. 'Water is alkaline which increases oxygen and abnormal (or ageing) cells do not survive in oxygen-rich environments.'

John Stirling is a biochemist who is in the process of developing a substance called TimeGuard which is both an oral and a topical (something you put on your skin) anti-ageing supplement agrees.

'There are a number of foods that help protect the skin against sun damage,' he says. 'Foods high in Beta carotene such as carrots, pumpkin, sweet potato (the orange variety) and tomato which is a good source of Lycopene. Beta carotene and Lycopene both reduce oxidative damage to the tissues.'

Stirling would add sardines to your daily diet because they are a good source of vitamin A and vitamin D; both necessary for skin health and a good way to reduce inflammation.

'Oily fish will help reduce inflammation,' he says. 'Which is also associated with over-exposure to the sun.'

Stirling also suggests stocking up on lots of vitamin C rich foods because they help strengthen connective tissue (a form of fibrous tissue of which collagen is the main protein) and prevent free radical damage. Mango, papaya, strawberries, blueberries, blackberries, black currants, oranges and lemons are all good.

rest of her body and face look 20 years younger than her hands.

'The gaps are extremely ageing, and effect very slim women more than others. But you are fine,' continues Dr Amir.

The really excellent news is that if I haven't got gaps now, the likelihood is that I won't ever. 'But there are wrinkles,' he says, his caress turning into a pinch. 'And the skin is getting very thin.'

Dr Amir suggests we do a Pixel session. This is a procedure which heats up the lower dermis of the skin, to the extent that it thinks it is being damaged, thus triggering a healing process which in turn means you end up with younger looking skin due to the increased collagen and elastin that is produced to heal the skin. What is so clever and different about this laser is that it's a fractional laser, meaning it doesn't cover the entire surface of the skin, rather it covers sections. Which is much less aggressive on your skin so it is not as painful and there is less downtime (downtime is the phrase used to describe the period after your treatment when you will look like a mad woman as your body/face/hands etc recover). But these sections are close enough to ensure that the regeneration process in the skin in between that is not lasered starts as well.

Dr Amir says I will see some difference after one session but that ideally I should do three or four with a time-span of four weeks between each session.

He also mentions in passing that he thinks I need my lips done. And that I have platismal bands around my neck. Great. I don't even know what they are, but apparently they can be got rid of with Botox. He gives me a mirror and tells me to speak. He's right, there are sinew-like things protruding on my neck. Happily I'm wearing a scarf, so I wrap that around it and we get back to the hands. I am beginning to find it odd how all these experts get to tell you what's wrong with you, a sort of 'no offence but your lips are too small' or 'have you ever thought about a facial peel?' And I'm not sure I needed to know about my platismal bands frankly. But now that I do know about them, I have to know more.

I ask Dr Amir if they're linked to ageing. 'Could be,' he says. 'Or you might just always have had them.'

Great, so I've been wandering around all these years with a serious defect and haven't even noticed.

Dr Amir's crisply-clad nurse leads to me a room where I will have some pain killing cream put on before the treatment. The whole of the clinic is white. It's a little bit like walking onto the set of a sci-fi film. Even Dr Amir's computer is white. It's actually quite hard to see where you're going with no points of reference. The place is utterly spotless and every member of staff looks impeccable. They are all Arab women with hair as long as my arms, vertiginous heels and masses of make-up. I start to feel a little dowdy as I walk through the clinic in my flats hiding my platismal bands.

A nurse covers my hands with cream and then puts some rather fetching blue rubber gloves on them. After 45 minutes I am led downstairs to where Dr Amir is waiting with the laser.

I sit down in a large leather chair. I have to wear rather strange-looking protective eye gear so I can't see a thing. For some reason I am reminded of the torture scene in Orwell's 1984. They could do anything to me they wanted to. My hands are numb and I'm blind. Dr Amir removes one of the rubber gloves and gets to work. He moves the laser systematically across the back of my hand, and presses something that makes it go click.

'Does it hurt?' he asks.

'No, not really,' I reply. 'I think I can smell the hairs on my hands burning though.'

It is not painful during the procedure, which lasts for about five minutes, but as soon as he has finished my right hand starts to feel extremely hot and uncomfortable. A nurse puts what feels like an oversized ice cube on my hand and rubs it around, which feels lovely. The left hand is soon finished and I can take off my eyewear. Both my hands have hundreds of tiny pinpricks in them.

'These spots will turn into scabs,' says Dr Amir. 'Do not remove them. I will give you some healing cream you should apply every four hours for four days and you need to put a tretinoin cream on at night. And of course you need to wear sunscreen every day.' Tretinoin cream is available on prescription only and reduces discolouration and uneven skin tone.

The nurse hands me the ice cube, which is in fact a surgical glove filled with ice. I constantly pat the tops of hands with it as I walk back to the hotel. I'm not sure where most of the heat is coming from, my hands or the Abu Dhabi air.

The next morning my hands are slightly swollen and the scabs are starting to appear. Putting hot water on my hands is really painful, and it's tough to wash my hair. I can begin to imagine what a serious burn must feel like.

It's a strange thing, this concept of tricking the skin into thinking it's being damaged so it produces more collagen. In fact we're not actually tricking it, the lower dermis is being damaged. And the evidence is there in the form of my swollen hands and tiny scabs. My husband thinks I'm nuts and just shakes his head when I show them to him, but I have faith in the Pixel. Although for the first two days after the treatment my hands look older than they ever have, all sort of burnt and leathery, really nasty. 'They look like they've been under the grill,' says my friend Carla when I get back to England. 'I can see the advertising slogan 'If you want your hands to look like grilled kippers and pay a fortune for it then come to us'.'

Four days later my hands still look like grilled kippers. There is one awful moment when Olivia my 15-year-old daughter goes to hold my hand and recoils in horror. The children then spend all weekend examining my hands and making faces. During a massage about a week after the treatment I noticed the massage man lifting up my hand to examine it. Again I had to explain what was going on. If I do a repeat treatment I might do it in the winter, when I can wear gloves.

In fact it's not until a full two weeks go by that they start to look normal. And then they begin to look better. I notice that the skin tone is more uniform. I'm sure with several treatments I would see more of a difference, and as Dr Amir pointed out, the results keep getting better as the months go by and skin regenerates, so maybe the best is still to come.

Whatever else, I now religiously put sunscreen on the backs of my hands to protect the work of the laser.

Moving down the body to our other extremity, our feet, we don't really pay them much attention, do we? Until they hurt, or we find an ingrowing toenail or stub our toe. Yet our feet are miraculous. They carry our weight day in and day out. They have 26 bones and 33 joints. And did you know that foot fetishism (also known as podophilia) is the most common form of sexual fetishism? I can't believe I've never even met anyone who showed any interest in my feet. I feel bereft. And what does a foot fetishist do anyway? There was that famous toe-sucking event with Fergie, but what else?

In any case, back to my non-sexualised feet. I love the quote from Oprah at the beginning of this chapter. If you invest in nothing else, spend money on good shoes. 'There's a time to save and a time to spend,' my stepmother says. Shoes are a time to spend. Nothing looks cheaper than cheap shoes, and your feet deserve more respect.

Obviously our feet age, like the rest of our bodies, but unlike our hands they spend most of their lives hidden away. Which is probably why we don't bother doing anything about them until it's suddenly time to wear a pair of flip-flops. Much like the rest of us, one of the results of ageing on our feet is dry skin. Try to get into the habit of lathering them in some kind of cream last thing at night (do this when you're actually in bed unless you want to risk skating across the bathroom floor).

Our feet are often called the mirror of health because illnesses such as diabetes show on them. If you've ever had reflexology you know how painful it is when the reflexologist touches the part of your foot that corresponds to for example your bad back or bad digestive system. Therefore, it's important to check your feet regularly or have them checked by a podiatrist (no I had never heard of one either but apparently they're easy to find and not all of them are perverts).

Keep circulation going by not sitting cross-legged or wearing shoes that are too tight. Walking is the best exercise for your feet, so walk as much as you can.

It goes without saying that if you don't have the time or money for regular pedicures then invest in a good pumice stone.

And if you do come across a podophile, ask him or her to give you a nice foot massage. It's very good for your feet and you will make both of you very happy…!

Here's one I tried: The elephant (elbows and knees) in the room

I first noticed a serious deterioration in my knees about a year ago when I was in France on holiday. It may have been the harsh sunlight, or possibly just the angle I caught them at, but as I looked at myself in the mirror before heading out to the beach I realised that a longer dress might be more flattering than the shorts I was wearing. My legs have always been slim and over the years I have exercised regularly to maintain their shape, ensuring I do something most days from walking to squats to yoga or cycling. The reason was my knees. There they were, looking wrinkly and tired, surrounded by saggy skin. They were almost incongruous with the rest of my legs. They looked, well, really old. There really was no other way to describe them. If they were looking old, I wondered, what state were my elbows in, the other area notoriously susceptible to sagging skin. I checked my elbows out, and soon wished I hadn't. I was developing the classic what is known in the trade as 'elephant elbows' where your skin is almost ruched or pleated, a bit like a piece of material. I was still slim and fairly young looking for my age, but these two areas were dead giveaways.

Most women know how to make the most of an ageing face. We use a careful skincare regime and sometimes more drastic measures such as peels or laser treatments. A well-stocked make-up bag can do wonders to hide some of the effects of the passing of time. And if all else fails, there's always Botox.

And then there's the body. Obviously the older we get the more effort we have to make to look anywhere close to how we did when we were in our twenties or thirties. For example, we have to pay more attention to what we eat; gone are the days when calories consumed seemed to just fall off, we need to exercise regularly. And it's no longer enough to take a stroll to the shops and call it done. As we age we need to really work at it, we need to use weights to maintain strength and form for example. I try to do three sessions a week with kettlebells involving everything from one-armed rows to sit-ups and bicep curls. I balance that out with yoga twice a week, which keeps you supple and your muscles stretched. So far this has worked well for most of my body.

But there are areas, such as your knees and your elbows, that are trickier to maintain, or disguise, and that can really let you down. The skin around the knees and elbows tends to sag rather more than elsewhere due to the fact that there is simply more of it, which of course gives the joints the cushioning and the flexibility they need to move. As we age the skin around the elbows and the knees deteriorates, just like it does everywhere else. There are things you can do to make it look better, such as regular moisturising and exfoliation, but in my case I felt more drastic measures were needed.

I had heard about threading before I tried it. And I'm not talking about the fairly innocuous kind that you have done to prune bushy eyebrows. No, this is the kind that involves inserting medical threads made of polydioxanone synthetic fibre into the skin and creating a kind of supportive mesh underneath it. A sort of secret lift I suppose you could call it. The threads dissolve over a period of six to eight months, but by this time they have encouraged the body to produce fresh collagen, elastin and hyaluronic acid, all of which of course slow the ageing process and we produce less and less as we age.

How they do this is a "mystery" says Dr Gabriela Mercik who first brought the thread lifts to the UK in 2013 and is considered the pioneer of them in the UK. "It is only the PDO (polydioxanone) threads that have this effect, no one knows why."

Dr Gabriela, who is originally from Poland where she was a heart and lung surgeon, worked in the NHS in Ireland treating breast cancer patients before she decided she wanted to focus on the cosmetic side of medicine and opened up her first clinic in London's Harley Street. She is now the main teaching doctor for threading in the UK, and travels around the world teaching the procedure. She is an energetic, warm woman who is clearly passionate about her work and whose mission it is to use her "miracle" treatment to make us all look younger.

"You should have your jawline lifted," she tells me and then rather helpfully takes a picture of my face side-on to show me that she means. "You don't see this, but other people do," she adds. 'Poor things' is the implication. I must look slightly crestfallen, as she pats my hand. "Don't worry, we can fix this, this is an easy procedure, and brings great results."

Today though we are all about the knees and the elbows. What makes this treatment so revolutionary is that it is able to treat two areas that are otherwise practically impossible to improve on, however much you exercise or whatever you do to them. Because no matter what you try, the knees and elbows remain stubbornly aged. Threading is the only thing that can affect them, but even that is not fool-proof.

"These are not the two areas that bring the best results of all the areas you can have lifted," says Dr Gabriela. And in case you're wondering, that is pretty much anywhere. Everything I mention from my Caesarean scar to my eyelids to my buttocks is greeted with a cheery 'we can fix that' that is slightly reminiscent of a dodgy builder. By the time Dr Gabriela has applied the numbing cream on my knees and elbows and wrapped them in cling-film I am slightly wondering if there is any part of my face or body that doesn't need "fixing".

I am left for half an hour to allow the cream to do its work. I'm also given a face mask that contains a hydrating serum, which apparently keeps your skin hydrated for 72 hours. Dr Gabriela's own brand skincare has received rave reviews and is based on keeping the skin moisturized through molecular water that transports hyaluronic acid deep into the skin.

Once the numbing cream has had time to work, Dr Gabriela begins with my left knee. This will be the most painful part of the treatment as the cream has had the least time to take effect. The method is as follows: a needle is inserted just under the surface of the skin that contains the PDO thread. Dr Gabriela weaves the threads together until they create a mesh that supports the skin, almost like a hammock, and lifts it. Dr

Gabriela injects the needles in an upwards direction in order to ensure the lift. Once they are in she twists them, which in turn creates a small knot that means the thread will stay in place inside the skin tissue.

Most of the needles go in pretty painlessly, which is pretty amazing, as they must be about two and a half inches long. There are times though when I feel them, and the twisting bit hurts sometimes. I would say around one on a pain scale of one to ten, but some of them are closer to four or five. Dr Gabriela inserts around 15 threads, I can see her assessing her work as she goes, a little like a sculptor creating the perfect form. She works quickly and efficiently. Some swelling is already starting and there is a little blood, but overall it's not too gory. The second knee is much less painful and by the time we get to my elbows I am completely numb.

Under normal circumstances Dr Gabriela would have let the cream stay on longer, but as I was being photographed we had to slightly rush things. If I had my time again though, I would have got there earlier and given myself more time to get properly numb.

The elbows are treated to a combination of filler and threading. The filler, which is injected, creates volume where there is none and the threads do what they will do to my knees; lift and encourage collagen production.

Dr Gabriela explains that she is using filler on my elbows because the skin there is dryer, more aged and there is not a lot of fat tissue.

"You will see the full results in about eight months' time," she tells me when the whole process is over. "Although the collagen will start to build after about two weeks."

It has to be said that when I leave the clinic I am not in the best possible shape. My face looks fresh, thanks to the hydrating mask, but my knees are swollen and sore, my elbows less so, I guess because they have had fewer needles. I hobble out clutching my bruise prevention cream, worrying that I may have caused myself permanent damage. I can barely bend my knees to walk normally, they feel so sore and vulnerable. My elbows are not as bad, but if I accidentally brush into something it hurts. I have tried a lot of treatments over the years and my husband keeps saying "one day you're going to do something really stupid." As I ease myself onto the train back home thanking my lucky stars that I got a seat I wonder if this is finally it.

For that first night after the treatment, I have been told to apply an abundance of the anti-bruising cream Dr Gabriela gave me and to wrap my knees and elbows in cling-film. As I lie there surveying my cling-film wrapped joints and my husband asks me if I am planning to become some kind of Christo-style art installation, I do wonder if I have finally lots the plot.

The following morning my knees are still bruised and sore. I cancel all my gym sessions for the week and rub on the anti-bruising cream regularly. There are bruises just above my elbows, but much less than the knees.

Over the next few days as the bruises seem to get worse. I do bruise very easily, but I look like I've been had a rather tortuous gardening session or been in some awful accident. Added to this there are periodic sharp twangs of pain rather like someone flicking an elastic band or a slight electric current going through my knees, especially when I walk.

The bruising stays for about a week, and the twangs decrease to almost none at all. But still now four weeks after the threading, I get the odd one.

The results are, as Dr Gabriela predicted, not massively dramatic. I am sure that if I ask any of my friends if they can see any difference most of them would say no. But then they probably hadn't ever really examined my knees and elbows in the first place. There is a difference for sure. It is least noticeable when I stand with my legs and arms totally straight. But even then there are less creases and both areas look less ravaged. But it is when I bend them ever so slightly that you see the real effects. I suddenly have the knees and elbows of a much younger woman. I am also aware that this is early days and that the effect will keep improving until it peaks this summer, just as the weather gets better and I can start to really show off my rejuvenated knees and elbows.

www.drgabriela.co.uk

Star product

What? Olaplex Hair Perfector

Why? Olaplex is a fabulous new product that rebuilds damaged hair. It works on a molecular level to mend the broken bonds thus making it look glossy and luscious. Or as my hairdresser Imran puts it: "Imagine the hair strand is a ladder with broken rungs, Olaplex restores the rungs." In salons they mix it with your colour to give you a glossy boost, but you can buy a variation for home use. The only slight hitch is that you need to put it on unwashed towel-dried hair, so I am writing this with my slightly wet hair covered in Olaplex, which will dry into a kind of mass before I wash it out. It should stay on for an absolute minimum of ten minutes but you can leave it on as long as you like. Once it has done its work it will stop. The effects are really noticeable. I have never much liked my hair and it seems to be getting stragglier with age, when I use the treatment it is much glossier and more manageable. It's not cheap though, I would say a bottle that costs £32 lasts around a couple of months.

Top Tip

Full-face threading: Threading is a process by which hairs are removed by trapping them between two twisted pieces of thread and pulling them out. Many people have used the technique to shape their eyebrows but I'd never considered having my entire face threaded. However, as we age, due to our increased testosterone levels hair sprouts in the most unseemly places. The face is one of them. I didn't even think about the fact that parts of my face was covered in a very light down until it was gone. I can't pretend the treatment was painless; think leg waxing and quadruple it, but the difference is incredible. My face looks more defined, my skin clearer and make-up glides on with ease. I have heard people say that taking out the fuzz can lead to darker hairs growing back but it's too soon to tell. I will most definitely keep going with full-face threading, a total revelation.

minxbeauty.com

Hand cream — never leave home without it

There are some things I never leave home without. Lip-gloss is one of them. Paper handkerchiefs is another. But one thing I hardly even leave my bedroom without is hand cream.

My hands seem to be endlessly dry. I imagine people will shake my hand and think 'yuk, she needs some moisturiser'. So I am constantly rubbing cream into them. This can be dangerous for driving. I sometimes find my cream-laden hands slipping on the steering wheel as I go to turn a corner. It also means I leave my fingerprints wherever I go. I would never get away with a burglary. The fingerprints I leave are visible to the naked eye.

This is not much of a worry though, as I am not planning any crimes. But what I have been searching for is a hand cream that lasts more than three minutes before I feel the urge to reach for the pot again.

Ever since Dr Amir in Abu Dhabi told me that it was very important to put sun block on my hands because sun spots develop easily on the backs of the hands. These are horrible things that give away your age as much as wrinkles on your neck.

To protect my hands during the day, I started to carry hand-cream and sun-block around with me. Then I had an epiphany. What about a hand cream with a sun block already in it? This would lessen the load in my handbag, which is having a bad effect on my ageing neck and shoulders.

There are several options on the market. Clarins is a nice one, as is the Neutrogena one. But the best one I have found so far is the Natura Bissé Tensolift Hand Cream. It is smooth, luxurious, deeply moisturizing and it lasts for several hours. After a few weeks of using it my one sun-spot even seems less obvious.

A friend of mine says she gives her hands a mini-facial once a week. This means exfoliating them, then putting them in a bowl of warm water with a drop of milk in it. Finally rub some oil on them. If you are really keen you can wear cotton gloves at night to help your skin to absorb the moisture. I have tried it and it works, but sleeping with gloves on was really strange. But at least I might not leave my fingerprints behind…

Star Product

What? Renouve anti-aging hand sanitizing lotion

Why? Much better for your hands than ones laced with harsh ingredients such as alcohol, this little gem uses bitter orange peel extract to cleanse and also contains peptides and antioxidants to firm and replenish. It smells lovely too.

Top tips for anti-ageing your hands

* Always wear sunscreen, even in the winter. Your hands are exposed to the sun more than any other part of your body. This is a habit to start in your twenties if possible and not once your hands are already aged
* Wear rubber gloves when washing up and handling detergents
* Wear gloves when driving to avoid harsh rays hitting your hands through the windscreen
* Moisturise as frequently as you can, and always after washing them. Try to use a cream that contains epidermal growth factors (EPGs, naturally occurring proteins that stimulate cells to multiply), as these have been shown to be especially effective when it comes to hands
* Exfoliate your hands once a week, this will help deter sunspots
* Exercise your fingers to avoid the onset of arthritis
* If your sunspots are really serious contact your dermatologist, they may be able to treat them with lasers.

8

Taller, younger lighter

'The main facts in human life are five: birth, food, sleep, love and death.'
E.M. Forster

There are many things I have thought about doing in Mayfair's South Molton Street, one of London's most exclusive shopping streets. Maybe pop into Browns to check out some clothes, or Space NK to scam some testers for the latest anti-ageing products. But little did I imagine myself lying on a treatment bed making snake-like sounds while an attractive woman with curly blonde hair prods my stomach.

I am here to learn how to breathe properly. The blonde lady is called Caroline Kremer and she uses a combination of her own methods and something called the Bowen Technique (named after Tom Bowen the Australian who invented it) to align your body so that your diaphragm has the freedom to breathe to its fullest capacity.

'We all live in fight or flight mode these days,' says Caroline, as she aligns my shoulders and tells me what's wrong with my posture. 'Messages on our phones, sudden panics at work, all these require a stress response. So we no longer breathe properly or use what I would call diaphragmatic breathing, our breathing is shallow and this is not good for us.'

Caroline tells me that on average a person takes about 16 breaths a minute, but that we should be aiming for closer to eight to 12 breaths a minute for good health and longevity.'

The difference between breathing fully and not is that when we breathe fully we are stimulating what is known as the parasympathetic nervous system, or what is known as our rest and digest system. The parasympathetic nervous system is the opposite of the sympathetic nervous system, which is all about the fight or flight aspect of our nervous system.

'So when we are faced with that tiger, and we need to run away from that tiger, the sympathetic nervous system comes into play and it gives you all of the energy, it directs everything to where you need it for an emergency,' Caroline explains. 'So that will shut down part of your digestive system, it will direct energy towards the main muscle groups, it will store fat around your middle because it believes that's where it is best placed to be used immediately. The problem is, wind forward several thousands of years and we are now dealing with daily stress and not just the odd tiger. We probably live in the most stressful time humanity has ever seen.'

What we need to do it to make our bodies realise that these stresses are not actually life-threatening, that we don't need to shut down all our systems to deal with a snotty email from our boss or a cracked phone screen. We need to breathe when small stresses hit us, as opposed to start hyper-ventilating and panicking.

'Even if it's a tiny thing, the body only has one way to respond to it,' she continues. 'So we dip down into the stress and come out of parasympathetic and when that stress disappears we come back up and then we dip a little bit back down into the rest and digest mode until the next stress hits us. So we come out of that and then we go right down into the stress mode. So we never actually put ourselves right down into the rest and digest aspect of our nervous system. We're constantly fighting against the other one.'

If we can master Caroline's technique the benefits are potentially numerous; increased energy levels, sleeping better, lower blood pressure, improved digestion, boosting your immunity, regular massages for your heart, even avoiding cancer. 'Cancer can't live in an oxygenated environment,' says Caroline. 'My husband died of cancer 15 years ago which is why I've got in to doing what I do now, I suddenly became interested in health and food and nutrition and what can we do for ourselves.'

Caroline is a strong advocate of exercise (especially yoga) and eating well. But up there with these two tools to keep us young and healthy is breathing in the manner we were born to breathe. Caroline estimates 99.9 per cent of people get it wrong.

'I want to just trigger a natural response from your body,' she says. 'The body already knew how to breathe before all of the stresses and strains came into it. For some this response means going back to childhood, for some that's not quite so far back as that.'

As I lie down in Caroline's treatment room it occurs to me that I may not have drawn a proper breath for almost half a century. Caroline starts with a combination of massaging and poking around on various parts of my body. This is to loosen the fascia, no I'd never heard of it either, but a loose fascia is crucial if we are to live well and breathe properly.

The fascia is a layer of connective tissue that looks a little like the plastic mesh you sometimes get on wine bottles. It is made of collagen and holds all your muscles, blood vessels and nerves in place. It can become brittle and hard if it's not stretched or exercised. Which is one of the reasons Caroline loves yoga, it loosens the fascia.

'When we go to bed at night we don't move around very much and the fascia becomes slightly gel-like, sort of a bit sticky. The reason why we stretch in the morning is to break that stickiness down to then free up movement.'

Caroline tells me to take a deep breath in through my nose and then to breathe out slowly through my mouth while making a hissing sound.

'Breathe out until you don't think you can breathe anymore and then keep going until you can feel your stomach muscles contract,' she tells me. I'm amazed at how long my out breath goes on for. There is a point where I really feel there is no breath left in me, but I find a final gasp. I feel like all the stale air right at the bottom of my lungs has been expelled.

'Good,' she says. 'Now breathe normally for a few breaths. I feel slightly light-headed.

'The air that we breathe only contains 21 per cent of the oxygen we need, the rest is other stuff, so we really need to be breathing properly to be getting that oxygen, especially when living in towns and cities,' says Caroline as she continues to manipulate my fascia.

She tells me to turn my palms upwards and to take another long breath in through my nose. I then repeat the hissing outbreath.

'Slow it down a little,' she says. 'Keep it even. If we exhale fully, then the inhalation is going to happen on its own because the body is going to demand it. The exercises were created around full exhalation and when you add the weights it's a little like lifting your arm while carrying a weight. Because what you're doing is you are pushing the air out under pressure and your diaphragm, as it relaxes and extends, is having to work at the same time.'

For the next breath I am told to put my arms out at shoulder height 'like an airplane'. By now I am getting the hang of this and can see that it could become addictive. I feel somewhere between rejuvenated and soporific, and cleansed.

'Breathing properly detoxifies the body,' says Caroline. 'So it's very important to drink plenty of water.'

Next I am asked to put my arms above my head and hold onto my elbows. Then to hug myself and repeat the breath. I notice that after one breath my arms seem to have got longer, in that I can hug myself more tightly.

'That's your fascia loosening,' Caroline tells me.

Caroline advises me to do these exercises at home in bed when I wake up. 'Take 10-15 minutes, and do six breaths each. Your breathing will have been shallow during the night, so take it easy on the first breath then build on it, this will energize you. Similarly if you can't sleep at night and you want to get to a place that is calm and relaxed then put two breath patterns in at night, this will relax you and help you sleep. It is slowing you heart rate, decreasing your blood pressure and a great way of toning your belly muscles! You're using all four layers of your abdominal muscles when you do the exercises.'

I stand up slowly and try to describe how I'm feeling. Certainly stronger, energized, taller, loose and relaxed. A whole combination of things. I am sure that this session will stay with me, and I am going to focus on breathing out when my phone pings as opposed to drawing breath in a half-panicked 'oh help who can that be' fashion. I ask Caroline how to ensure we keep breathing.

'It is about having an awareness, starting to create an awareness of what your breathing is doing and what your body is doing. When you walk down the street, how are you walking?

Can you feel the movement going all the way to your head when you take that step? Does it feel fluid? And then you can take that awareness into your breathing and you can ask yourself, 'Where do I feel the breath in my body?' It's just a question of getting your body used to it and realigning. So we need to understand and have freedom through the body, which is when you have good alignment. This work is all about having optimal alignment for where you are in your life.'

Caroline walks downstairs with me. Her next client is waiting for her, a man in his forties who looks stressed and hurried. I can imagine he will look very different by the time she's finished with him. I thank her and tell her I feel great.

'The three most common words I hear from clients are taller, younger, lighter,' says Caroline.

If breathing properly can achieve all that and much more, you'd be a fool not to try it.

Ageing, no longer a superficial issue

There are top scientists taking it extremely seriously. Forget the face creams and the liposuction, we are talking about the biological reasons we age and how to stop the process from happening. Not only stop the process, but start becoming biologically younger.

Calico, or California Life Company, is a biotech company founded by Google in 2013 to tackle the process of ageing. The plan is to use the latest technology available to increase the human lifespan by understanding the biology behind ageing and to eliminate age-related diseases such as Alzheimer's.

Calico is the US equivalent of what is more or less a one-man band on this side of the Atlantic, the formidable Dr Aubrey de Grey, a Cambridge PhD graduate and gerontologist who runs SENS (Strategies for Engineered Negligible Senescence), a research foundation specialising in rejuvenation treatments.

When I first met Aubrey back in 2007 he told me that he believed the first person that was going to live to be 1000 years old had already been born. Aubrey de Grey argues that ageing is merely a disease, and a curable one at that.

'When I talk about defeating ageing I mean ending the correlation between how old you are and how likely you are to die,' he says.

He says that in his lifetime he expects to see a world where 90 year olds will be as healthy as 50 year olds. 'It's not just about life, it's about healthy life,' he says.

He concludes that humans age in seven ways, and that we can avoid all of them. He calls them the 'Seven deadly things' and they include things like nuclear DNA damage, failing adaptive immune system and the build up of senescent cells.

To deal with these seven deadly things de Grey suggests adopting what he calls the engineering approach. 'Let's go in and repair all these various types of damage so that we keep the level of damage down to below the threshold that must exist that causes it to be pathogenic,' he says. 'We already know how to fix them all in mice, this is our Robust Mouse Rejuvenation (RMR) work, and in some cases in humans. If we can get decent funding we can probably develop robust rejuvenation in all areas for humans in about 10 years.'

At the moment, our lifespan is increasing by two years every decade. De Grey wants to see it increase by a year every year. He also predicts that the first person to live to 1000 is only 10 years behind the first person who will live to 150. And that, at least, does not seem so far away.

Beauty sleep

I have a long wrinkle down the right-hand side of my face that I know now I could have avoided. It is the worst wrinkle of my face. It starts around my mouth area and works its way up to my eyes like a thin meandering stream. Once there, it splits into hundreds of other tiny that form the collection of wrinkles around my right eye.

This wrinkle is at its worst in the morning, because I have slept on that side of my face. And as any anti-ageing expert will tell you, the way to avoid wrinkles like this one is to sleep on your back. I do know this. And if I happen to wake up in the middle of the night and find myself on my side (as I invariably do) I quickly move onto my back in the vain hope that I am not increasing the depth of the hideous wrinkle that some mornings is even more prominent than my nose.

What I should have invested in several years ago is a silk pillow-case. I finally have one. It sits on my bed like it's waiting for some royal head to lie down on it. It looks beautiful, it is beautiful, and comfortable. Not to mention luxurious. And silk pillowcases are apparently the only way to avoid sleep-induced wrinkles. So now I can sometimes sneak onto my side and not panic about that wrinkle getting even worse. Although I really have left it too late. Considering by the time we're 60 we will have spent around 20 years with our heads on a pillow, it might be worth investing in a silk pillowcase immediately! And while you're at it, Egyptian cotton sheets. I once stayed with a very rich friend who had these on his bed, it was like sleeping in a cloud. I'm sure the mattress and pillows were 100 per cent duck feathers too, or whatever the most exclusive thing is.

Of course it is not only how you sleep but how well you sleep that affects how you age. The term 'beauty sleep' is not just an empty phrase. According to research commissioned by Estée Lauder and carried out at University Hospitals Case Medical Centre in Cleveland Ohio sleeping badly can accelerate the skin's ageing process. Added to which the skin is less able to recover after sun exposure if you haven't slept well. A sample of 60 women aged between 30 and 49 were analysed, with half of them not getting enough sleep. Scientists used tests such as UV light exposure to check for moisture loss, skin slackening, uneven skin colour and fine lines.

Dr Elma Baron who ran the study sums up the results: 'While chronic sleep deprivation has been linked to medical problems such as obesity, diabetes, cancer and immune deficiency, its effects on skin function have previously been unknown. Sleep-deprived women show signs of premature skin ageing and a decrease in their skin's ability to recover after sun exposure.'

Janet Lord, the Birmingham University professor quoted earlier in the book, says we must redefine our notions of how much sleep we need. I am obsessed with getting eight hours sleep a night. Professor Lord says that's too much. 'The optimum amount of sleep time for good health seems to be around 5 and a half to six and a half hours,' she says. 'Studies have shown that people who sleep for less than five hours a night have the highest risk of mortality, and the perfect amount seems to be less than the seven hours we all thought it was.'

Several years ago I interviewed the supermodel Inès de la Fressange. For those of you who haven't heard of her, she was probably one of the first supermodels there was, and a Chanel muse for many years. In fact, she recently made her catwalk comeback at a Chanel show, now aged 50-something. I talked to Inès about facials and she said she didn't believe in them. What she did believe in, however, was the restorative benefits of the sleep she would have while having a facial.

She is right about the benefits of sleep (although I would argue a good facial is not to be underestimated). During restful sleep our skin cells regenerate at twice the speed they do when we're awake. According to a study published in the *British Medical Journal* 94 per cent of women said a good night's sleep was the best tonic for looking good.

So how do we ensure it? I am a self-confessed sleep Nazi. I can't bear to wake anyone up and if I am woken up myself I go into paroxysms of despair. Purely because I find it so difficult to get back to sleep. And then I stress about not getting back to sleep and of course don't get back to sleep and so it goes on. There are a few things that help:

Breathe deeply. Deep breathing will help, in part because you're so busy focusing on your breathing that you don't have time to get stressed about the fact that you're awake in the middle of the night.

Don't smoke. If you're a smoker then there is really no point in reading this book at all, because you're willingly exposing your skin to the second most damaging thing there is bar the sun. But in terms of sleep, remember that smokers are four times less likely to feel rested after a night's sleep in part because nicotine is a stimulant and also because smoking itself exacerbates breathing disorders, which lead to disturbed sleep.

Exercise. But try to keep it around three to four hours away from bedtime to reap the post workout melatonin-induced benefits.

Avoid caffeine after 3pm. Have a decaf after dinner instead. If you're English and need that afternoon cup of tea then have it (I do) but limit it to one cup. And NO coffee.

Prepare well. Have a lovely lavender bath, do some gentle stretching, go to bed fully cleansed and pure ready for that invaluable cell-restoring rest.

Convert your concerns. By which I mean those 3am worries such as 'did I post that letter'? 'How will I pay that bill'? Write down constructive steps to deal with these issues. And/or breathe and focus on your breath and watch them go away. Really these are all things that can be dealt with and should not be keeping you awake at night. Remember Mark Twain's quote: 'I have spent most of my life worrying about things that never happened.'

Listen to music/ a book/ a relax app. This again will take your mind off your worries about things that will never happen.

Don't overheat. A warm bath before bed is a good idea as it sends s signal to the body to produce melatonin, which helps you sleep. But for a good night's sleep you should be closer to cool than to hot. Remember to turn off that heated blanket. Especially if you're menopausal — disaster!

Create the perfect ambiance by spraying some sleep-inducing scent. I love the Deep Sleep Pillow Spray by This Works for example. I also sprinkle lavender oil drops all over my bed after I've made it. Chamomile and ylang-ylang also do the job.

White noise — if you live somewhere particularly raucous then opt for some white noise to help you tune out. When I lived in the Middle East I found the hum of the AC was extremely good for blocking out noises from the street. If you don't need AC there are plenty of apps that produce a low-level calming sound.

Eliminate light. I rarely sleep beyond 7am but when I do it is always in a hotel room with floor to ceiling protection from light. I grew up in Sweden and I remember those white nights (when it is light all night) being impossible. Light sends an incredibly powerful signal to your brain to wake up, even if it's from a phone or a laptop. Glows from electrical devices can pass through your closed eyelids and retinas to your hypothalamus and give your brain the signal that it's time to wake up.

Be aware of your spine and neck. Ideally they should be in a straight line to avoid tension or cramps. If our neck is raised then get a better pillow. If you sleep on your stomach then you might be better off without one.

Don't panic! If you wake up stay put, breathe, visualize, listen to a relax app. If you really can't get back to sleep then get up, do some yoga, or just some stretching, write down all the things that are buzzing around in your brain and then go back to bed. Above all stay calm. You will survive, even if you don't get eight hours' sleep every night.

Star Product

What? Neal's Yard Lavender Bath Salts

Why? This is one of my favourite products ever. There is nothing quite as comforting after a long hard day as a bath with this lavender oil infused sea salt combo. The smell is divine. You feel cleansed, soothed and moisturised after the bath, added to which the whole rooms smells like a field in Provence. Heavenly!

9

It's all in the detail...

'There are no ugly women, just lazy women.'
Coco Chanel

I have guarded my long hair like a national treasure for as long as I remember. Nothing could persuade me to part with it. In fact, I spent most of 2008 adding to it with hugely long hair extensions that made me look like a WAG. Looking back on it I must have been insane. It's enough trouble looking after your own hair, let alone someone else's.

As part of writing this book I have taken it off. I don't know if it's a sign of maturity. I had what I can only describe as a bad hair month. No, it was longer than a month. Or at least it felt like it. I would wash my hair, and blow dry it, and then tie it up in a scrunchie. Because it invariably looked bloody awful: Thin, unhealthy, straggly just hideous. And I couldn't bear to see it lankly hanging there. I tried everything to revive it from covering it in oil overnight to conditioning treatments to not washing it for a few days in the hope that it would suddenly spring back into life. It didn't. And one day I realised that I really hated my hair. That it was making me ugly. In fact, it was making me look OLD. It just had to go.

This revelation came to me in Virginia Water. But rather than wait until I got back to anywhere near a hairdresser I knew and trusted, I needed immediate gratification. You just can't have that Eureka moment and then leave your hair for another minute. It's like suddenly deciding you want to chuck your boyfriend and then sleeping with him again.

So I stomped off to a local little hairdresser called Mova and asked if they could fit me in immediately. Yes, Sophie would be with me in a couple of minutes the receptionist told me.

'I don't know if I'm going through the menopause, or what's going on,' I told a horrified looking Sophie minutes later as I settled into the chair. 'But I just HATE my hair, it just hangs there looking hideous. Can you cut it off please?'

I realised at the time that I was demanding what most women really want when they go to the hairdresser's; a total and utter transformation. And that they are hard to come by. But it was worth a try.

Luckily Sophie was one of those salt-of-the-earth types who make me wonder how we ever lost the empire. She took it all in her stride and we agreed on a short bob, a conditioning treatment, roots colour and a blow dry.

There was one slightly panicky point when she twisted my long hair into a ponytail and said 'I'm just going to get rid of some of the length, it will make it easier to cut. Are you sure about this?' But then I remembered how much I loathed my hair and told her to go for it.

Grooming is a huge part of staying young looking and within that hair has got to be the most significant aspect.

As Sandy, a Tasmanian hairdresser friend of mine puts it:

'Hair is your 24 hour accessory. You're never fully dressed without great hair.'

I describe my bad hair month to Sandy and ask her if it is just my imagination that my hair is ageing.

'Absolutely not! It is strongly related to hormones, just like so much else when you age. As you age and your hormones change, your hair changes.'

'So I have to deal with the hormones?'

'Yes but you can also help delay your hair getting worse by looking after it. And how you treat it will depend on the changes it is going through. Everyone's hair will change in a different way, some hair will go oily, some dry, some people's hair will fall out and it needs treating accordingly.'

Whatever the problems with your hair, Sandy says you need to look at both internal and external ways to treat them. 'Hair only lives internally, it's dead on the outside, so you have to treat it internally,' she says. For example, better diet, drinking more water or hormone replacement therapy could all be internal treatments.

For external treatments one of her top tips is massaging the scalp, which stimulates the scalp, blood flow, and the regrowth of dormant hair cells.

Another top tip is brushing your hair. 'There is an old wives' tale that says brush your hair a hundred times a day. It may be an old wives' tale but it works for the simple reason that if you're brushing it properly you're massaging the scalp. Added to which, your natural oils sit on the scalp so brushing it gets the natural oils from the roots to the ends of the hair and there is no better nourishment for your hair then your own natural oils. I say to people if their hair isn't growing, try to brush it before you go to bed, let the natural oils sit on your hair, and wash it in the morning. It's a really good (free) treatment.'

Even though your hair is dead, it can of course be treated on the outside to increase lustre and condition, which will make it look healthier and of course younger. You can condition it, cut it, colour it, blow-dry it and so forth. What you are doing with conditioning treatments is combatting the effects of ageing on the hair by smoothing the cuticle thus reducing the horrid frizzy look of ageing hair, in turn a result of your hair becoming increasingly coarser as it ages and goes grey.

The most obvious effect of ageing is of course grey hair. The bad news is that this starts in your thirties. The good news is that your pubes may never go grey at all! Although I noticed a grey eyebrow the other day, which I am sure bodes badly. And a grey underarm hair. How that little bugger had managed to make it there I don't know. I had my underarms, bikini line and legs all lasered years ago.

Talking of the past, a couple of years ago my first love showed up at a dinner party I was at. This is a man I met when I was a teenager, fell madly in love with and then lost touch with for a couple of decades. We lost touch, yes, but of course that doesn't mean I didn't think about him. First love never dies, and I am living proof of that. Or at least I am living proof of another saying; There's no fool like an old fool.

Over that dinner he looked deep into my eyes. 'Help,' I thought. 'Is he about to tell me he made a terrible mistake all those years ago and has thought of little but me ever since?'

'Do you dye your hair?' he asked.

'No,' I lied, before adding. 'But you should dye yours.'

Grey hair is hideously ageing. I know that there are some women (my mother among them) who just let it come on and don't worry about it. They can even look very elegant. I have a French friend who carries of the grey look with total aplomb. Helen Mirren of course looks totally gorgeous, as did

Meryl Streep in *The Devil Wears Prada*. A (male) friend of my mother's has white hair and was once asked why he doesn't dye it. 'I do,' he replied. 'I dye it this colour.'

Sandy says that if you are lucky enough to have that gorgeous white-grey hair like the head of the IMF Christine Lagarde you have hit upon the one and only upside to ageing hair. She estimates that without dying my hair I would be around 50 per cent grey. But of course there is no way I can tell if I have lucked out in the white-grey hair stakes because I don't leave my hair long enough to see what kind of grey colour it is.

According to Sandy the way to test it is to leave a patch at the back of your head without dye for a couple of months and see what it looks like. If you then discover you are the 'right' sort of grey you need to start the painful process of growing it out. While it's growing you put in dark and blonde highlights to avoid that awful roots line. Then you gradually do less and less highlights.

I suggest to Sandy I want to wait at least another ten years before I embark on that route.

'I think you should,' she replies, 'but what you have done by cutting your hair off is good. As we get older things change, our bodies change for example, so we change our clothes. But people forget to change their hair. They come into the salon and complain that their hair doesn't do what it used to do. Well it's not the same hair! You have to change your hair in order to adapt to that. For example, if it's got thinner you've got to have a cut that gives it more body.'

Robert Chambers, the Dublin-based celebrity hairdresser, agrees with Sandy. 'Women should in general wait until they are in their seventies to go grey,' Sandy tells me. 'Otherwise it can be terribly ageing. And another good tip for those 'in between times' is to make your parting a zigzag. That will hide the grey and also give your hair more body.'

Robert has a mane of rather glorious curly grey hair that is shoulder length. He says he has some lowlight and highlights through it, and I must say it looks like a work of art. He describes himself as 'a man in a woman's world' and has been transforming women since he started cutting hair as an apprentice in Dublin in the 1960s. 'Women often ask me if I can take 10 years off them, I tell them I can take off 15!' he says. 'I believe a great haircut that can be worn casually is best. Less is more! Particularly, as you get older, a less structured look I think is best to make you look younger. Also I would warn women and men against dying their hair at home. You really are taking a risk with both the results and the condition of your hair if you do that. It's very hard to tell from a packet what will suit your skin tone. As you age your hair and clothes need to make you feel confident, as well as younger than your years.'

Of course he would say that about going to a hairdresser's to get your hair dyed because he is one, but I have to admit that dyeing my hair at home has never worked very well. It looks incredibly fake and the condition afterwards is terrible.

I meet a fabulous Italian hairdresser called Gabriele Cipriani. He is terribly dramatic and extremely passionate about women, in a way that only a gay man can be. 'The face is like a painting,' he says, 'and the hair is like a frame. So if they are both the same colour you can't see either of them.' So his theory is that if you have a yellow skin pigment, you can't be blonde because you would look like a ghost. 'There is nothing worse in the life,' he tells me. I can but nod and agree.

Gabriele divides the ageing process for women into three phases. Up until the age of 25 you can basically get away with anything; long hair, short hair, bright red hair, whatever you want. From 25 to 55 you have to be as natural as possible, otherwise you will look older than you really are. And from 55 until the end you need to do something to refresh your hair, maybe cut it shorter or dye it a lighter shade. 'Older skin needs a lighter colour,' says Gabriele. 'And if you have a lot of grey hair a lighter colour makes maintenance easier too.'

Just as our skin ages, so does our hair. We need to moisturise it more and pay more attention to it. The older we get the more body and moisture our hair loses. The oil glands shrink with age and produce less oil, hence the lack of shine and moisture, and the diameter of your hair gets smaller so you have less body. If like me you have very thin, dry hair to begin with, it's a disaster.

There are a few things you can do of course to lessen the drastic effect of ageing on your hair. Again you need to eat well, and as your hair is made up of mainly protein try to include some protein in your diet. Try to use a night scalp mask once a month, and a moisturising mask before shampooing once a week or so.

L'Oréal has announced that it will be launching a pill to stop hair going grey. Sadly for those of us who are already part of the way there, it is not going to reverse the process, but it will halt it.

Sandy told me about a scalp treatment massage from Kéraste called Densifique that apparently stimulates your dormant hair cells and will add around 1700 hairs to your head within three months.

Geraldine Howard, the founder of Aromatherapy Associates, says that hair-care is the only area of where you need to use non-natural products. In order to create the shiny hair we all crave, you have to use silicone. 'We're working on a natural alternative,' she says. 'But it's difficult.'

My top tip is to have a sharp new haircut. Sophie did a great job and I left the salon feeling very perky with my Anna Wintour bob. I also think that as we age we need to accept the fact that we have to take more care of our hair and that we have to invest more in it. A few years ago I would never have spent money on getting my hair blow-dried. But now it makes such a difference to the way it looks.

Finally, I just want to mention stray hairs. Not many of us will look attractive with a great big black hair sticking out of their nostril. OK so you may not need to get your nose hairs waxed (and yes I do since you ask, you have to go to a barber's shop where they will put wax on a Q-tip and whip them out!) but they are easily trimmed to be neat and inside your nose.

Can you believe that while all the other hair on our head and bodies gets weaker and lighter with age, random hairs on our chins get darker and stronger. Great. Yet another bonus to ageing. Keep some tweezers with you at all times, and the best place to spot them is in the rear-view mirror of your car on a bright sunny day.

Nails are very much linked to our hair, and as we age they too become more brittle and dry. Another really unpleasant side effect of ageing is that your toenails become much thicker, I have no idea why, but it's very unattractive. There are a few tips to help ageing nails look their best:

* Only file nails in one direction
* Every evening before bed massage oil into your 20 nails, wheatgerm oil is ideal, or jojoba oil. You will notice a massive difference after just a few days
* You can also soak your nails in olive oil for 10-15 minutes a day. Try this for a month and see what a difference it makes. After the initial month you can reduce it to once a week
* Limit how often you use nail varnish remover, it is extremely drying
* Limit exposure to harsh detergents and cleaning

materials by wearing rubber gloves
* Always moisturise your hands (and nails) after contact
  with water
* Eat biotin rich foods such as eggs and avocados
* Don't cut your cuticles, soften them with warm water
  and push them back.

Star Product

What? Percy & Reed Wonder Treatment + Oil.

Why? I love pre-shampoo products, but what is fabulous about this little gem is that it can be used both pre and post treatment. You can either rub it into dry hair before you wash and style, or you can use it on towel-dried hair, working the oil from your scalp down to ends of your hair. Either way it increases gloss and shine, as well as protects and, according to the blurb, rejuvenates your hair with Carrot Seed Oil. I'm totally sold on it. I saw an instant straw to silk transformation.

Top Tip

I have been involved with false hair since I was a teenager. I had the Haysi Fantayzee look for months. Then a decade or so on I had masses of extensions applied by a madman in New York that made me look like a WAG only with smaller boobs.
I am pleased to announce that hair extensions have finally come of age. My lovely hairdresser, Imran at Michealjohn in Knightsbridge, has started a new subtle approach with extensions especially aimed at women who have either thin or thinning hair, or who just need a volume boost. They are incredibly low maintenance and blend into your own hair imperceptibly. I love them. My hair is actually easier to style and

look after with them than without. And bad hair days are a thing of the past.

www.michaeljohn.co.uk

Silver foxes

Dying my hair was one of the first things I ever did to fight the ageing process.

I was in my late thirties when the first bits of grey poked through. I remember being livid. As well as shocked. Surely I wasn't that old? How dare my hair start to go grey?

I immediately made an appointment with my hairdresser and ever since that day more than eight years ago I have been dying it every few weeks to cover any sign of grey.

We women are not like our male counterparts who can go grey with impunity. When their locks turn grey they are called silver foxes, as opposed to aged or over the hill. Take the Great British Bake Off judge Paul Hollywood for example. Does anyone expect him to dye his hair? There would probably be a national outcry if he did. Richard Gere is seen as distinguished with his grey locks, as is George Clooney, a man who has probably done more to make grey hair on men something sexy than anyone else.

But for women it's a very different story. Glossy, youthful hair is the very essence of our femininity. We must dye our hair at the first hint of silver, and not stop until we drop. Nothing says I've given up like grey.

My hair has been through different guises over the years; it's been blue, it's been pink, I've had extensions, I've even had fake dreadlocks, but one thing I have never had, or even contemplated having, is grey hair.

Until now.

I am not a woman who is timid about changing her hairstyle.

But this is without doubt the craziest thing I have ever done.

At my age (late–forties since you ask), most women (and some men) spend their time trying not to go grey. But this has all changed. Grey, at least in terms of hair colour, is the new black, or blonde.

As is so often the case, it started with a slew of celebrities (the majority of them under 30) who decided silver was the way forward. Rihanna, Lady Gaga, Demi Moore, Cara Delavigne, Stella Tennant, Kylie Jenner, the list goes on. Suddenly grey (or silver as my stylist Imran at micheljohn prefers to call it "grey sounds so negative") hair has become just another colour choice.

It might in part be explained by the 'old is the new young' zeitgeist. Suddenly being old has become trendy. The style icon Iris Apfel is gracing our TV screens and the FT's How to Spend it Magazine cover at the age of 90. Paul Young has made a comeback at the age of 60. Suddenly our television heroines are no longer twenty-somethings, but women with gravitas and grey (ish) hair such as Mary Beard and Mary Berry.

Ours has always been a terribly ageist society. But as the ageing population slowly takes over, we have to adapt. We are going to be a nation of oldies with silver hair before long. By 2050 half the population of our cities will be over 60. Within 20 years half the population of Western Europe will be aged over 50.

Now that being aged is going to be the norm, even fashion has to adapt.

So for me, today, silver is the colour of choice.

Going silver is not for the faint-hearted, or those on a tight schedule. And it is definitely not something you should try at home. The process is more complicated than dying your hair any other colour because before you can even think about creating silver streaks, your hair has to be lifted. This lifting entails removing your pigmentation until your hair is basically neutral in colour.

"We have to lift it to a very pale blonde in order to get silver," Imran explains. "If the colour is not clean enough the silver will look slightly orange or muddy."

Imran adores the new silver look, but says you need to "embrace it" in order for it to work. "You need to make a statement," he says. "Demi Moore just looks like she was kind of scared to do it and so didn't do enough."

As Imran mixes peroxide and puts my hair in foils all around my face, I am beginning to have a certain amount of sympathy for Demi. Surely with grey (sorry, silver) I can't help but look older? I have written two anti-ageing books, and nowhere in either of them do I advise women to let their hair go grey, let alone dye it that colour.

"I wouldn't recommend doing the whole head in your case," says Imran, "but to do some streaks around the face. This will create interest and soften the roots. I think the lighter tones around your face will really soften your look."

It has never occurred to me to dye my hair any other colour than the one I was born with. Apparently that's where I've been going wrong.

"As you age, your skin lightens and if you don't lighten your hair then it just doesn't work," Imran explains. "I never understand women of a certain age with jet-black hair, it just looks wrong. They think that just because they had that colour when they were young, keeping that colour will make them look young again. It's a common mistake."

My hair is not jet-black, and never was, but it is dark brown. I have also never gone in for highlights, so this whole foils thing is new to me.

"The adventure begins," says Imran, busily mixing colour and folding bits of silver foil into my hair. After about 40 minutes I have a ring of silver around my face.

"A little preview," he jokes, and puts a heated contraption over my head that will apparently speed up the lifting process. Just as well, because if it needs doing twice I could be here for another two hours. Already the estimated time it is going to take to turn me into a silver fox is three to four hours.

Hair dye has possibly been the most revolutionary anti-ageing tool of the last decade. "There's a reason why forty, fifty, and sixty don't look the way they used to," Nora Ephron wrote in her book *I Feel Bad About My Neck*, "and it's not because of feminism, or better living through exercise. It's because of hair dye. In the 1950s only seven per cent of American women dyed their hair; today there are parts of Manhattan and Los Angeles where there are no grey-haired women at all."

British women typically start going grey around the age of 33, and they stop trying to cover it up on average aged 68. That's over 30 years of dying their hair. No wonder the home hair dye market was worth a staggering £322 million last year. We spend an annual £7.2 billion a year on hairdressers in the UK.

This silver trend has been one of the quickest to catch on. Thousands of attractive young women are giving a whole new meaning to the term silver fox. In May 2015 Amazon sales of grey hair dye soared by a staggering 83 per cent.

"It started on the catwalks and filtered down," says Imran.

What is incredible is the amount of under thirties adopting it, turning grey or silver hair into the latest must-have really rather edgy accessory, almost like a tattoo. On Instagram they use #grannyhair to show off their styles. There are almost 200,000 posts. For #silverhair there are close to 550,000.

They look fabulous. I'm not surprised it's caught on, there is something incredibly sleek and sexy about the silver look.

Of course there are older women turning silver too, in part because it makes their lives easier. "For those women it's not about making a fashion statement," explains Imran. "They do it to cover up re-growth so they don't need to dye their hair as often" Into this category fall elegant examples like Christine Lagarde, Managing Director of the IMF, the actress Helen Mirren and the FT's Business Editor Sarah Gordon.

Gordon writes in a piece in the FT about her experience that going fully silver is not a low-maintenance choice. "I have realised that a sharp cut and great condition are a pre-requisite for looking good with white hair."

I think the full-on grey is a very brave choice, only really for the very glamorous or the very grannyish. Cara Delavigne, who has been credited with starting this trend on the catwalk, looked great. Rihanna looks amazing. My mother, who has a full head of silver hair, looks incredibly glamorous. But it's a big call.

I think though we all have to accept that sooner or later, block colour just doesn't work any more. As Imran says, just because you were a raven-haired beauty when you were 20 doesn't mean you should keep that same hair colour as you age.

There is nothing more jarring than a woman who can't possibly have grey-free hair having grey-free hair. There does, after all, come a point when that conker-brown brunette or dazzling blonde do is just, well, clearly not natural. I have a female relation in her eighties who still dyes her hair dark brown. It's not a good look. Eventually we have to soften the dye job, but for a lot of women that cut-off point is tricky to negotiate.

This is where this new trend for silverlights or 'half-way highlights' (ie half-way between a complete dye job and a wiry mass of grey) is so brilliant. It's a totally new look that says 'I embrace my age but can still look glossy and glamorous'. It's a kind of half-way house between full-on colour and full-on grey, and administered carefully can effectively bridge the gap between the two for as many years as needed.

Of course stripping your hair of its natural pigmentation is never going to be good for it, and this is one of my main concerns when I decided to have this treatment. Will I end up with grey, straggly hair that not only makes me look I've seen better days, but has clearly seen better days itself?

Imran reassures me by telling me he uses a revolutionary new product called Olaplex that builds up the hair. "Anything from heat to even something as simple as brushing it can damage your hair," he says. "If you think of your hair strands as a broken ladder, what Olaplex does is to rebuild that ladder with false steps. I am adding Olaplex to the peroxide to protect the hair we are dying and then I'll add it to the rest as well just to boost the condition."

Imran agrees that silver hair is harder to maintain than other colours. "Warm colours do shine more. And you never see wild silver hair that looks good, you really have to style it out."

In between blow dries for models appearing at London fashion week Imran checks my foils.

"It's lifting nicely," he says a few times. "Another ten minutes."

Rather like a manicure where the preparation is the time-consuming thing and the nail varnish goes on in a matter of minutes, the lifting here is what takes the time. Once it's complete Imran takes out the foils and as I look in the mirror I am reminded of my 16-year old self when I bleached my hair with cheap peroxide. I look hideous. But before I can run screaming from the salon, Imran has installed me at the basin in a chair that rather brilliantly gives you massages.

The next step is to put the silver colour in. "It will take quite quickly," says Imran. "Now that your colour is down to this porous neutral tone."

I spend about half an hour with my body being massaged by the chair and my head being massaged by Imran. Then it's time for the blow-dry. This is the bit that always worries me, because I know I won't be able to do it at home. My post-washing routine usually consists of rough drying my hair at best and sometimes using straighteners to smooth it out. I watch Imran working with a round brush and the hairdryer and make a mental note to up my game.

Finally, we're done. I look in the mirror. At first, the result is slightly shocking. I am grey. Grey equals old. This is not good. But then I look again; there is a new life to my hair, a new movement, there is definitely some "interest" as Imran put it earlier. Actually my new look makes the old block colour I had seem rather drab.

Imran is delighted with the result. "It's elegant, sharp and chic," he says. "I love it."

I leave Imran to have lunch with a friend I was at university with. At first she doesn't seem to notice, but when I tell her she has a good look, even lifting up bits of hair to examine it.

"I wouldn't have had such a big bit right at the front," she says. "But it looks good."

It's true that one normally feels more chipper after a trip to the hairdresser's but as I leave lunch to go to a business meeting I feel really good. Rather than making me feel grey and less confident, the silver streaks make me feel more attractive. As Imran said, you have to make a statement with them to make it work, to make it look like something you've made a conscious decision to do as opposed to just letting it happen.

There is no way I could naturally have these silver streaks; it's clear I have had them put there on purpose. With my silver streaks I am embracing my age as opposed to hiding from it. I am a woman of a certain age and not ashamed of it. For the time ever I am admitting to the world that I'm middle aged and it feels like a relief. No one seems to think less of me for it, least of all a business associate I meet later that day who tells me I look fabulous.

My teenage daughters, however, are harder to please. "Why didn't you have your whole head done," they both wail.

"You look almost as sexy as your mother," says my ever-helpful husband.

Three days in and I am a convert. I have even managed to wash my hair and although it doesn't look quite as good as it did when Imran dried it, the silver is still lively and engaging.

After a few days the family are converted too. "I agree it lightens up your face," says my husband. The girls treat me like a kind of circus animal, telling any friends who come round to "check out my mum's silver streaks." So far they have been unanimously approved of. In an Instagram and Facebook poll I carried out, 80 per cent were for them.

www.michaeljohn.co.uk

The dazzling smile

It all started with a university friend I hadn't seen for many years. We were sitting opposite each other at the wedding of a mutual friend. There was something different about her. Had she dyed her hair? Undoubtedly. At our age if you don't you end up looking like your grandmother. Had she lost weight? No, she was still quite a big girl. But she looked great, in fact dazzling. And then it struck me; it was her teeth. They were whiter than George Clooney's. I was mesmerized by them. I just couldn't stop staring. Finally, being an investigative journalist, I decided I had to pluck up the courage to ask her about it.

'Your teeth look great,' I ventured. 'Were they always that white?'

She smiled that dazzling smile.

'No, of course not, but I have been living in Los Angeles for the last ten years,' she replied. 'And I don't want people to be able to tell I'm English by the state of my teeth.'

A fact I was not aware of until this fortuitous meeting was that the English are (in)famous across the globe (but especially in America) for having bad teeth. And when I say bad, I don't mean rotting and falling out over lunch, but yellow. Or 'natural' we might call them. But apparently no one in Los Angeles has natural teeth any more, and why would you when you can look like a Hollywood film star.

So I began to investigate. I started with the soft stuff; teeth whitening toothpaste. It made no difference at all as far as I could see. Although it did make my teeth feel clean.

Next I tried the home whitening kits, some more complicated than others, but all of which involved putting a paste of some kind on my teeth and leaving it to work its magic. I saw a little bit of a result but not too much. One of these kits is one your dentist has to prepare for you, where they make an impression of your teeth that looks a bit like a mouth guard and you wear at night with teeth-whitening substance plastered on your teeth — horribly uncomfortable but slightly more effective than the shop-bought ones.

Then I went to New York on a business trip. I happened to know the PR person in charge of one of New York's premier teeth whiteners, a certain Dr Theodorou, and she set up an appointment for me.

I cannot pretend that teeth whitening in a pleasant experience. For a start you are not allowed to eat or drink anything with any colour in it for 24 hours; so that means no wine (red or white), no coffee, no tea, no food apart from white bread (no crusts) the list goes on. Added to which I was subjected to a contraption that would have made Hannibal Lecter squirm for 40 minutes; a kind of rubber brace that kept my lips away from my teeth and my mouth wide open. Every 10 minutes or so Dr Theodorou would come in and put some paste on my teeth. I watched *Lost in Translation* during the whole episode, which happily is one of my favourite things. I did need something to take my mind off the goings-on around my mouth.

The results though, were incredible. And 40 minutes of slight discomfort were nothing if you think that in those 40 minutes, 40 years of eating and drinking were being wiped away. My teeth were as dazzling as my friend's from LA. I couldn't stop smiling. I almost walked into a lamppost while admiring my grin in a shop window. It really is one of the most effective anti-ageing mechanisms out there. Without resorting to the surgeon's knife I looked several years younger. And in only 24 hours I could have a glass of champagne to celebrate.

Top Tip

Once a week give your hair a nourishing overnight treatment using an oil such as the Aromatherapy Associates Rose Oil, the ila-spa Body Oil for Inner Peace, or even just plain olive oil. Rub it into your hair the day before you're going to wash it and leave it to work overnight. Wash thoroughly the following day.

Protect your hair dye

There are some things you can do to maintain your hair dye for as long as possible. First do not wash your hair with shampoo for two days after you've had it dyed. And when you do wash it, use cool water, hair dye hates heat (so avoid hairdryers too if you possibly can). Use a shampoo that protects colour and also a protecting serum such as L'Oréal's Paris ELVIVE Colour-Protect Reflecting Serum. Avoid the sun and chlorine in pools (some hope if you live in the Middle East). And even before you have it dyed get it into tip-top shape by using conditioning treatments. Healthy hair stays coloured for longer, apparently.

You don't need to do all your roots every time you get your hair dyed. For example just go for the so-called T-section, the parting, that should buy you another two weeks or so. And use root cover-up such as Wow.

Star Product

What? Color Wow Root Cover Up

Why? This has now become one of my 'I can't live without' products. Finally an answer to unsightly (read GREY) roots that seem to pitch up literally minutes after I've had my hair dyed. This little magical invention means I don't have to go the hairdresser's every two weeks.

Star treatment — permanent eye make-up

I have discovered tattoos. No, I do not want to look like David Beckham, nor indeed have I gone for a subtle (or even not so subtle) tramp-stamp as they have become known at the top of my buttocks. In fact, anything like that makes me extremely nervous.

When I say tattoos I mean the sort that make you look better; I am talking about permanent make-up. I have had black eye-liner tattooed onto my eye-lids. This does not look as 'Cruella de Vil' as it sounds. It is extremely subtle, a thin line just at the very edge where my eye-lashes start, but it has an incredible effect. It makes my eyes appear wide awake, whatever state of somnolence they may be in. I can actually go out without make-up on, well, OK I would still put some lip gloss on. If I am going out at night, I add another line with an eye-liner pencil and suddenly I am Audrey Hepburn. For me, the best thing about the permanent option is that I don't have to be reminded of the crinkly state of my eyelids every time I try to put some eyeliner on.

Going back to the lips. According to my permanent make-up guru Candice, I could of course have them done as well. There are several options; permanent lip-liner, or lip-liner with a bit of shading.

Anyone with dodgy eye-brows can solve their problems with permanent make-up, it is completely miraculous what they can do. I have a friend who shaved her eyebrows off when she was 13 and they never grew back. Don't ask me why she shaved them off, but she did. For years she walked around with a ridiculous line drawn over her eyes where her brows should have been. Now she has eyebrows that would make Cara Delevingne sit up and take notice.

Of course they call it permanent, but it isn't really. It lasts for about two years. Which is still a lot longer than any normal make-up, especially lip gloss, which I find myself reapplying about 20 times a day. Maybe I should try the permanent option after all?

Star product

What? Sisley Phyto-Lip Twist.

Why? A few times a year you come across a product that you really wonder how you ever lived without. This new Sisley lip gloss is just such a product. Part nourishing, part beautifying and all gloss, I came across it by accident as I was looking for stocking fillers for myself on behalf of my husband. I have been faithful to the Clarins Instant Light Lip Reflector for almost two years. But it was time to move on. The Phyto-Lip Twist almost melts on, leaving lips supple, moisturised, slightly plumped and luminous. I have never been one for a lot of colour on my lips so went for number 1 called Nude. Then I went back for another because I loved it so much. Having tried every colour there was I opted for Balm, number 16, which is see-through. The oversized pencil itself is not the prettiest, but you soon get over that once you fall for its effects.

Top tips for dressing
from personal stylist Gabrielle Teare

* The older we get, the more structure we need. Don't be tempted to wear clothes simply because they're comfortable. They won't do you any favours. As Karl Lagerfeld says: 'Sweatpants are a sign of defeat. You lost control of your life so you bought some sweatpants.' Go for structure every time
* Invest in some key pieces. One day you will be 70 and when are you going to get that great wardrobe? Instead of buying seven jackets from Zara, buy one really great one
* Be positive and make the very best of what you've got
* Remember we make decisions about people in the first twenty seconds of meeting them and dressing well is a crucial part of that first impression
* Accessorise well; appropriate but not flashy. Wear memorable shoes. Buy less but better
* Don't be intimidated by rules. Tina Turner is a granny and wears short skirts, and she looks great in them
* Don't put on too much weight, once you are over a size 14 the choice of what you can wear becomes limited
* It's not about age; it's about making an effort
* Don't be influenced by the English attitude of 'we don't do glamour'. Of course we do

* Don't let your clothes take centre stage — they should complement your character and personality, not take it over
* Remember that a colour can add ten years to you or take 10 years off. Don't discard a colour just because you've never worn it
* Don't ever reach the point when you stop trying new things
* Anything that makes you look skinny and feel confident is the way to go. Avoid anything that doesn't

10

Child's play

'One should never make one's debut in a scandal. One should reserve that to give interest to one's old age.'
Oscar Wilde

We are going to be a nation of oldies. By 2050 half the population of our cities will be over 60. Within 20 years half the population of Western Europe will be aged over 50. Only Africa will remain a young continent, and that's because people still die young due to disease and malnutrition in parts of the continent.

This population shift will have a huge effect on society, healthcare, the workforce, pensions and much more. And one of the institutions set up to research this issue is the Oxford Institute of Population Ageing.

The institute is housed in the basement of one of those large North Oxford houses you can only really afford once you're old and have become very rich. It stands in a leafy road as you drive in from the affluent area of Summertown to the centre of Oxford. The vast house was obviously once home to a rich Oxford professor or the like, but is now split between the institute and a language school where foreign students pay fortunes to master the English language.

As I wait to meet its director, Professor Harper, I sit down on a sofa. I put my handbag down and spot a grey hair. Not one of mine, they are not allowed to stay grey for long enough to fall out. On the walls around me there are pictures of old people being cared for.

The institute was set up in 1998 to research the issue of population change, or in other words our ever-expanding ageing population. I am shown into a room where Sarah Harper, Director of the Institute and Professor of Gerontology and Senior Research Fellow Nuffield College, is waiting for me with a sandwich lunch. She is an extremely elegant woman, with bobbed brown hair and impeccable clothes. Her smile is broad and confident and she greets me warmly. We sit down and I let her do the talking as I tuck into a delicious vegetarian sandwich.

'The key thing is that a tremendous change in society lies ahead,' she says. 'It's not just that we're living longer, but we're having fewer children. Therefore, the median age starts to move up.'

Of course this means we won't be able to retire as early as we used to, because there won't be enough young people around to pay for our retirement. But according to Professor Harper, we probably won't want to anyway.

'Men and women in their 50s and 60s are still very active in the labour market,' she continues. 'If you think about it, if you're going to live to 100, you really can't retire at 60.'

Yes 40 years pottering around in my slippers doesn't sound too appealing. The trick though is to get employers to accept so called 'healthy later age adults' and actually give them jobs. I have worked as a headhunter and there is no one more ageist than a potential employer. Anyone over 50 is more or less written off. This has to change if her predictions are correct.

Professor Harper talks a lot about retraining, and people

having more than one career, for example leaving a career as an accountant in your forties to retrain as a teacher for example. She sees no reason why people can't have a second coming aged between 55 and 75. A bit like the late bloomers I mention in chapter one. In fact the job market will actually start to need people of this age to work, because there simply won't be enough people to keep things going if they don't. And more importantly, society can't possibly afford to support them.

'We also need to think about reassessing the structures we live by now, maybe education isn't something that just happens when you're young, maybe we need to be thinking about lifelong education, about retraining every few years,' says Professor Harper.

But this will only be possible if this increasingly ageing population looks after itself. There are some stark statistics out there and this particular one concerns men. A man aged 65 in the lower socioeconomic group has on average another 11 years of good health. A man of the same age in the higher socioeconomic group can expect to live healthily for another 22. Clearly the latter man is doing something that means he stays healthy (and alive) for longer. So it is within our control. We don't have to sit back and wait for ill health and incapacity to engulf us. We can fight back.

According to Birmingham Professor Janet Lord, one of our main tools is to move. 'No other species is sedentary in old age, it's a very human thing,' she says. 'You don't see it in other primates, they don't slow down with age, for example a monkey's climbing ability doesn't reduce with age.' I for one love the idea of senescent monkeys swinging from trees like lunatics.

Part of the reason we tend to slow down is evolutionary. 'We were really only meant to live to about 30-35 years old, long enough to have children and pass our genes on,' says Professor

Lord. 'Then between around 1750 and 1780 life expectancy started to increase. And now it is increasing at two years per decade. So the life expectancy of a child born today is five hours longer than that of a child born yesterday.'

The average life expectancy now in the UK is 80; 82 for a woman and 77 for a man. But, says Professor Lord, although we are living longer, we are not living healthier.

'On average now a female is unwell for the last 10 years of her life and a male is unwell for the last seven years of his life,' she says. 'So what we need to be doing is to get to a stage where people reach old age in good health. And it's not rocket science, it's all about diet and exercise.'

We have looked at both in earlier chapters but just to recap; move as much as you can, even if you're only capable of chair-based movement, move. Walk up any stairs you see. Do some housework. In terms of diet, remember the idea of reducing your calorific intake, which leads to a longer and healthier life, the 'eat less, live longer' mantra. Professor Lord tells me drug companies are working on a pill that will give you the same response as eating less. According to her they are 'quite close' and clinical trials on humans are likely to start in 'five to ten years' time'.

I have always said that what people who read a book like this really want is a magic pill that will fix everything without them having to actually make the effort to diet, and it looks like it's not that far away.

A stand-up marathon

At the moment, only two per cent of the NHS's budget goes into preventing people from being unhealthy as they age. There is not nearly enough investment in getting the message out there that staying fit (as well as alive) is the key to a happy rather than sickly old age. 'The current focus is on treatment,' says

Professor Lord. 'But the government has at least clicked and realised that it needs to start putting money into prevention. For example, we're trying to work with care homes to ensure that once people get there they don't just sit around all day, they do some kind of exercise, even if it's just standing up! Did you know that if you stand up for just three hours a day, you burn the same number of calories as you would running ten marathons a year. And if you stand up all day at work, for example if you work in a shop, you burn 400 calories.'

Professor Lord is in fact going to invest in a standing desk. It has a button that you can press if you want to lower it to sit down. I might have to get one too. Ernest Hemingway of course wrote standing up, but sadly that didn't help his longevity, but only because he killed himself.

Professor Sarah Harper says 'in order to be happy at 100, you have to be healthy'. The message from both these scientists is very much that we need to invest in our own futures by looking after ourselves from an early age. In fact, Dr Anna Phillips, Reader in Behavioural Medicine at Birmingham University, takes it one step further and suggests we need to be looking after ourselves from the moment we are conceived. 'Foetal nutrition is essential,' she says. OK so there's not much we can personally do about it, but we can at least look after our unborn babies.

The future seems to indicate that 60 will soon be the new 40. This is lucky as my son (aged 11) is constantly giving me a hard time, telling me I had him too late and that I will be ancient by the time he is an adult. It now appears that, on the contrary, I will be in my prime!

'You look at a photograph taken in the 1930s of a family with a mother and teenage daughter,' says Professor Harper. 'In those days the mother looked ancient. If you look at a picture nowadays the mother looks more like her teenage daughter.'

There are also some upsides to ageing. Yes, really. 'We get less good at things requiring speed as we age,' explains Professor Harper. 'But we have far better intuition and also our emphatic intelligence (our ability to empathise with people) improves with age. Added to which, creative people often produce their best work at an advanced age. A lot of critics far prefer Picasso's late work to his earlier work, and Matisse did some incredible things towards the end of his life.'

The professional view seems to be that, at least those who are in the higher socioeconomic groups, will not start to slow down until they are 80. And even then, they can expect to be healthy and active. Assuming they have been active up until that point. Professor Harper tells the story of two people she met, one aged 92 and the other 96 who were both in a deep depression; one because he couldn't play tennis any more and the other because he could no longer have sex. 'It doesn't matter what age frailty hits you,' she says. 'It's still a shock.'

An interesting statistic Professor Harper quotes is that if you are healthy at 70, you are more than likely to live until you're 100. And it is in society's (as well as our own) interest to stop us from degenerating, because as soon frailty and illness sets in we start to cost society money. And as we've seen if you want to actually live (that is move and have a life as opposed to sit like a vegetable in front of crap TV all day) you need to work at it, at least a little bit. At least until that magical pill comes out.

The application of science

You will be relieved to hear that tucked away in an impossible to find place among a myriad of Oxford University buildings there is a woman who is working tirelessly to make you live longer. Or at least to improve the quality of your cells so that you can live a healthier life.

Dr Lynne Cox, George Moody Fellow and Tutor in

Biochemistry studies the molecular basis of human ageing, with the aim of reducing the ill effects of old age. 'The first thing we have to do is to define what ageing is,' she tells me. 'Because it is one of those things that everyone thinks they know about, but no one really knows what it is beyond the very utilitarian definition that it is a progressive loss of function until death.'

Dr Cox is young, pretty and slim. She looks like she'd be as comfortable working at a fashion magazine as she is in the Department of Biochemistry at Oxford University. She is incredibly passionate about her work and tries her best to simplify it for me. Not an easy task.

'We've got this horrendous situation at the moment where life expectancy is going up but health expectancy isn't,' she tells me as we settle into her tidy, light office. 'What we are trying to do is to increase the health-span, not the lifespan. I always talk about adding life to the years, not years to the life. If you're old, ill and miserable those extra years just drag on and on.'

Dr Cox explains that your average female will be ill for the last 11 years of her life. 'Those years are generally just a combination of diseases. People think of ageing as wrinkles and grey hair, you can do stuff about that. But you can't do much about being incontinent or having leg ulcers that don't heal.'

Do I know what the NHS does about ulcers? No, but I have a feeling I'm about to find out.

'They scrape them off every few weeks and then put maggots on them to eat the dead flesh.'

Great, that's something to look forward to.

'The question is, should we treat the things that kill us such as dementia, cancer, cardiovascular disease, or look at the underlying causes?' asks Dr Cox. 'If you can treat what happens to cause it all, before you get the full-blown disease, you can stop the illness. And the process that we believe is going wrong happens right down at the level of the individual cells.'

As cells grow old they grow senescent, they lose the ability to proliferate. If you cut yourself your cells run around to heal you, to fill the gap. If you're old, they can't fill the gap. Hence the non-healing ulcers.

The reason we age is cells, or rather what Dr Cox called 'senescent cells', that is ageing cells. When we are young our cells are strong and healthy, they have long telomeres (telomeres are tiny caps on the end of chromosomes that protect the chromosome from ageing, think of them as the ends of shoe-laces fraying as they get older) and their DNA is intact. As we age the telomeres shorten and the DNA become damaged. This in turn means they can't divide or replenish. 'They lose their integrity and their function,' explains Dr Cox. 'When they're young under a microscope they're really very lovely, but the older they get the more debris they accumulate and they get all lumpy and bumpy and rather ugly.'

Dr Cox takes me into her lab, where she is growing cells. I feel like I'm on Grey's Anatomy as I put my light blue protective gear on. 'Don't touch anything,' she warns me. We compare young cells and old cells under the microscope. 'The young cells are beautiful. But they deteriorate and with that deterioration come a lot of damage, which causes inflammation and all sorts of problems that affect not only your health but also the way you look.'

So as your cells grow ragged around the edges, so do you.

When we talk about ageing cells, we're not talking about actual chronological age but rather the amount of times they have divided. Normal cells divide around 50 or 60 times though some skin cells can complete around 90 divisions. 'What we are trying to do here,' continues Dr Cox, 'is to delay the onset of senescence and in the end to get rid of senescent cells. Because if you can get rid of senescent cells then your tissue starts to rejuvenate.'

The basic premise is to reduce our biological age, or at least start to understand the causes of biological ageing in order to do something positive about it. 'If you know what's going on to make the cell old, can you interfere with that process? And what is the outcome? Well yes you can and the outcome is actually hugely exciting,' says Dr Cox.

She is positively brimming over with the prospect of what she might discover and be able to achieve with her research. But while we wait for this brilliant woman to devise a way of keeping our cells young, there are things we can do to help ourselves, or rather our cells.

Dr Cox quotes a study that compared mothers with disabled children to mothers of the same age with able-bodied children. The mothers of the disabled children had much shorter telomeres than the other mothers. 'The study shows how stress affects the ageing of our cells,' says Dr Cox. 'So it is crucial to avoid stress or try to reduce by for example doing yoga. In addition, an improved diet and doing more exercise can not only prevent telomere loss but has been shown to lead to a small but significant increase in telomere length.'

There are possible miracle cures on the horizon, among them Rapamycin, an antibiotic found in the soil on Easter Island, which has major effects beyond just being an antibiotic. When it is given to late middle-aged mice it extends their life by the human equivalent of 10 years. Experiments have also found that the drug has a positive effect in the brain, for example on Parkinson's Disease. Human trials are expected to start in the near future and there is already massive interest in Rapamycin from the global pharmaceutical companies.

But isn't messing with our cells, trying to change the natural paths they take a little like playing God? 'If you were diagnosed with cancer, would you not want your doctor to play God? Those are cells in your body that are aberrant, that are doing something they shouldn't do. Ageing is not something that used to happen to many people. Life expectancy used to be 40 or 50; population ageing is a modern thing. So we didn't have to deal with senescent cells. If you say it's perfectly fine to treat cancer because these are cells that have gone wrong, and you want to get rid of them, I don't see then that it's wrong to treat senescent cells.'

At the moment looking after our ageing population suffering from diseases and hideous ailments such as non-healing ulcers costs the NHS around 60 billion pounds per year. The government is beginning to realise that it can't possibly afford this increasing burden. Hence there is a lot of interest in Dr Cox's research.

'The last few years of life for so many old people are just dreadful,' says Dr Cox. 'And these are all people like us but a little bit further down the line. What we're trying to do is to complement this increasing life span with an increasing health span.'

She walks me to my car so we can keep talking before she has to dash off to give a lecture. 'We're not going to stop ageing but to make the process nicer,' she smiles as we say goodbye.

On behalf of all the senescent cells out there, I'm right behind her.

The menopause — Q & A with Dr Jennifer Landa

Dr Jennifer Landa specialises in helping women and men balance their hormones, restore their energy, and replenish their sex lives. At the heart of her practice is the belief that maintaining one's health is hard work and she encourages her patients to make lifestyle changes that will result in increased health. Dr Landa lectures on preventative medicine and has appeared on several television stations. She just completed her first book with co-author Virginia Hopkins. Their book, *The Sex Drive Solution for Women*, is a no-nonsense approach to many of the sex drive issues that Dr Landa addresses with her patients every day.

After a decade working as a traditional Ob/Gyn, Dr. Landa realised she wanted more for her patients and that her patients needed more from her. She spent two years becoming certified in Preventive and Regenerative Medicine, with an emphasis on bioidentical hormones and nutrition. Her winning combination of western medicine and alternative therapies has revolution-ized the way she practices medicine. Dr. Landa's mission is to teach her patients how to reach their personal best in optimal health and beauty using the most natural and advanced therapies available.

How do you know when you are peri-menopausal or menopausal?
The actual definition of menopause is one year without menses, so the difference is really very simple. Peri-menopause is the period surrounding menopause, which can last for one year. Unfortunately, this difference is not as meaningful as you might think. Many women have hormone levels that appear peri-menopausal and even sometimes menopausal in their twenties or thirties so it is much more important to have your hormone

levels measured and to receive advice to balance hormones based on your individual hormone levels.

What is your view on HRT?
I am heartily in favour of HRT as long as it is bioidentical hormone therapy. Bioidentical hormone therapy involves using hormones that are exactly the same chemical structure as hormones that are natural to the body. These are made from natural sources like soy and yams. These hormones can be tailored by a compounding pharmacist to address individual women's hormone needs. I prefer this type of therapy over traditional hormone therapies such as Prempro which has been proven to be unsafe in scientific trials.

What steps can women take to make the menopause less unpleasant and disruptive? For example is soya milk a good idea for oestrogen levels? Exercise?
Natural methods to balance hormones that can be helpful would definitely include exercise, getting adequate sleep, eating a nutritious diet of balanced foods and reducing stress. Some supplements like black cohosh might be helpful. I would not use soya milk or other processed soya products as these may be associated with excessively high oestrogen levels, although unprocessed soya products like edamame can be helpful and not harmful.

How can women increase their libido in later years? Why does it reduce so drastically?
One of the main reasons why women's libido is reduced in later years is because of the drastic drop in hormones that occurs after menopause. To have a strong libido it's important to have adequate levels of oestrogen, progesterone and testosterone and these levels must be well balanced. Many women suffer

from low levels of these hormones, which can decrease not only their libido but their ability to lose weight, have stable moods and good energy. Other contributors to poor libido in women at any age include poor mental health and difficulties in their relationships. Finally, problems with self-image cause many women to avoid sexual encounters as well.

11

Move it

'Of all the causes which conspire to render the life of a man short and miserable, none having greater influence than the want of proper exercise.'
Dr William Buchan, 18th century Scottish doctor

Recently I heard two nonagenarian ladies talking about ageing. One was on Woman's Hour. 'I used to enjoy gardening,' said the lady. 'I would love nothing more than to bend down and do some weeding in my flowerbeds, but if I try it now, I fear I may never get up again.'

The second lady is called Tao Porchon Lynch, she is a 96 year old who teaches yoga in New York. Never mind being able to bend down, this lady can stand on her head, put her legs behind her ears and is fitter and more flexible than most of her students. 'Yoga is a joining of our mind, body and spirit,' she says. 'It is like nature, everything is always recycled and brought full circle. I find I can heal myself if I do what nature does.'

The difference? I don't think the frustrated gardener has done a day's yoga in her life. Who knows if she ever exercised at all, apart from her gardening when she was still able to. The yoga teacher of course has done little else. She has been practicing yoga for over 70 years.

I am crazy about yoga, I try to do yoga every day but if yoga is not your thing then find something else that you do like. But you have to move. Exercise is the first key to ageing well. Think about it. Ageing is the deterioration of your body. So exercising stalls or slows down that deterioration. If you work a muscle, it stays fit. The example the 96-year-old yoga teacher is just perfect. She can still move because *she never stopped moving*.

Of all the anti-ageing tips and tricks I have researched I would say that exercise is the most crucial. Because you can have as many facelifts as you like and dye your hair as black as your hat, but there's not much point in it if you can't move is there? What do you think looks more ageing? The odd wrinkle, or someone stooped over a walking frame?

So the bad news is you do need to exercise. You should do something every day, even if it's just going for a walk. But most days try to do something more than that. The rather good news though is that you don't need to exercise that much.

According to Professor Janet Lord, Director of the MRC-ARUK Centre for Musculoskeletal Ageing Research at the University of Birmingham, the amount of time people move is split into three categories. First you have the sedentary group, which is people who do less than 30 minutes of exercise a day. Second is the moderately active group, people who do at least 30 minutes a day, be it walking to the shops or walking up stairs. Finally there is the active group, which would include amateur cyclists and other more 'sporty' types.

'The interesting thing is,' says Professor Lord, 'that you see the biggest difference between the first two groups. There really isn't that much difference between being moderately and really active. You get the best bang for your buck by being in the middle group.'

Professor Lord's message is this: 'Any chance you have to take a step, take it!' This can be something like parking your car a little further away to ensure a longer walk, or simply taking the stairs instead of the lift. Or if you do take an escalator, then walk up it. Moving is crucial as we age because it slows down all the negatives such as inflammation, muscle loss, loss of bone density and the thickening of your arteries.

'No other species is sedentary with age,' says Professor Lord. 'Monkeys still swing from trees, mice still scurry around, they don't slow down. What do we do? As soon as we are grandparents, and for some members of the Asian community here in Birmingham that can be at 45 years old, we sit down and expect to be waited on hand and foot. Then they gain weight and find it harder to move. And then what old people do is they move into bungalows, with no stairs! It's crazy. Stair climbing is amazing, it burns as many calories minute to minute as jogging.'

So just how much exercise do we need to do to stay fit as we age? 'You should do 150 minutes of some sort of aerobic exercise a week,' says Professor Lord. 'Along with that four sessions of resistance work. Now this doesn't have to mean going to the gym, it can be gardening, vigorous housework such as hoovering or walking or as I am always saying just going up and down stairs, which will help your bones as well. I always tell my elders if you can walk up and down a flight of stairs ten times a day it will have an amazing effect. Not only does it keep you fit but it will protect you from osteoporosis. In fact if you do nothing else then please do that! Just standing up helps too, we all sit far too much. If you stand up all day you burn 400 calories. If you stand up for more than three hours every day, you burn the same amount of calories as you would if you ran 10 marathons a year.'

The message from Professor Lord is very much that you can control (up to a certain point of course) how well or badly you age. She cites the example of a triumvirate of famous 76 year olds; Sophia Loren, Brigitte Bardot and Elizabeth Taylor. They were all born within weeks of each other, had the same occupation and the same number of husbands. But if you compare them when they were 76, they were extremely different.

'Liz sadly didn't make it beyond 76, she was wheelchair bound for the last few years of her life. Brigitte OK she has wrinkles but she's still physically active and Sophia, she's just incredible. I find that with the elderly people I deal with those that are still exercising are far and away in the best shape and still have that attitude of old always being ten years older than they are now.'

Professor Lord's advice is not to take ageing lying down, or literally sitting down. 'That attitude of "right, I'm 65 now, I'm retiring, putting on my cardigan and sitting down" is not going to get you anywhere.'

I think that you have to get the idea that exercise involves actually just exercising out of your mind and just look at most things as an opportunity to move. Psychologists Alia Crum and Ellen Langer recently published a study of chambermaids in the US. The job was typically badly paid by hotels and the maids were not highly motivated. When asked whether they considered themselves physically active, curiously most of the women didn't think they were. In fact, their daily activity exceeded the recommended exercise for healthy living. Even more curiously, their bodies showed no sign either of benefiting from their active lives. However, when the maids were told that the kind of work they were doing was the equivalent of doing several aerobics classes a week, their attitude and bodies changed measurably. Within a month they lost weight, were more positive and happier, even their blood pressure dropped by 10%.

So, from now on, when you're bending down to empty the dishwasher, think of it as stretching. Look at your own routines and think of them as your own daily exercise and increase the load a little where you can.

I love yoga because I feel it deals with my body and my mind at the same time. I get a sense of well-being from doing yoga that I don't have if I just jump around or lift weights. Although I am beginning to get hooked on that as well. I also find yoga incredibly effective for toning, which is the main thing at my age. There is an awful lot of strength work involved, just try holding a plank for a minute and feel every muscle in your body working. My friend Carla McKay (a novelist and author of *The Reluctant Yogi*) claims she can hold one for two minutes, but I so don't believe her! For more on her thoughts on yoga, please see her contribution at the end of this chapter.

If I don't have time to do a whole yoga session I just do what my yoga teacher Ria told me to do; get on the mat and do some poses that you feel like doing. Even if you only do ten minutes of whatever form of exercise you are going to make your own, it will make a difference. And some days you'll be able to do more, which will make more of a difference. Quite apart from the fact that exercise can reverse the physical symptoms of ageing (muscle loss, lack of bone density, decreasing metabolism, reduced flexibility and balance) it is also good for your mental health. It decreases stress (which as we all know is one of the most ageing things there is) and boosts your mood, as well as slowing down cognitive decline and the onset of dementia.

I use the Steps app that tells me how many steps I have taken a day. My target is 10,000, which is quite tough but doable, especially if you're out shopping. Our feet were made for walking, and that's exactly what they should do. If you get a bus to work then get off a stop before your destination. Maybe it will only be a five-minute walk but if you do that twice a day it soon adds up. Just try to add a few more steps wherever you can and you'll have an exercise regime that runs itself. Caroline Kremer who teaches the Caroline Kremer method told me the story of an aunt of hers who put all the things she regularly needs in the kitchen just out of reach, so that she really had to move and stretch to get to them. She was still active and mobile well into her nineties. Take a step here and there all day every day whenever you can and at the end of the week it will have accumulated into a significant amount of walking.

The most common excuse for not exercising is time. Can you spare ten minutes? Fine, if that's all you can spare then do ten minutes a day. An investment banker friend of mine who is almost 50 (and one of the few men I know of that age with a six-pack) does a ten-minute routine every day wherever he happens to be. He just rolls out of bed and gets on with it, which is much the best thing. Just do it before you have a chance to think of an excuse not to. As you can imagine his routine involves mainly sit-ups, but it keeps him in great shape. He also does press-ups.

If you need inspiration, there are literally hundreds of five or ten minute workouts online or in app form, focusing on whatever part of the body you like, or offering general all-round workouts. I like Freeletics for example. Do you watch television? Football matches? I do yoga, lift weights and do squats in front of the TV (if I'm not ironing, again good exercise). I'm not saying you have to become fanatical, but if time is an issue then use it wisely and exercise whenever you have a moment. There are lots of times I really do not feel like rolling out my yoga mat and getting the ipad set up to whatever workout I am planning to do. But as soon as I begin, I'm glad I did.

There is nothing like exercising to make you want to exercise more. You feel better, you have more energy and best of all, you look better. I met a fabulous trainer called Dan Buda a couple of years ago and he has transformed my body shape and attitude towards exercise. It does mean hard work to see significant change, but two half hour sessions a week have been enough to make me feel stronger than I have for years and look more toned too. When I started to train with Dan I had never ever done a full press-up. I could just about manage five on my knees. Two years on and I can do 20 full press-ups in one go. My sessions with Dan combined with my yoga have meant that I actually feel and look better as I get older and not worse. I am extremely grateful to him for showing me how important it is to invest in your own health in order to age happily.

Exercise is something that you can never stop of course. Because while it does not take long to start toning, it doesn't take long to lose that tone once you stop. I recently saw a programme about Victoria's Secrets models or 'Angels'. OK, they're young and stunning and their bodies are temples but they WORK at it: for several hours every day. So what's to stop us all becoming angels? Apart from the fact that no one is paying for us to stay in shape or model underwear but you get my point. I am so sick of people just giving up before they've even started to try to change their body shape with the old 'Oh I'm just not built like that' excuse. Those models wouldn't be paid the thousands of pounds they are paid if their bodies weren't absolutely perfect and guess what? They wouldn't be perfect if they didn't work at it. There's even a DVD called Train Like an Angel.

The toy-boy as an anti-ageing tool

I can't pretend to have done much research in this area personally, but my mother for one is a firm believer in toy-boys as anti-ageing aids.

'How can you feel old and unattractive when a young man still wants to sleep with you?' is her argument.

You only have to look at the effect Rudolf Nureyev had on Margot Fonteyn's career and persona to understand the benefits of having a younger man around. OK so he was famously gay, but the rumour is they did have an affair, and some even believe she was pregnant by him at one stage.

A friend of mine who used to live in France came back to England after her (French) husband divorced her. She was 45 years old at the time and they had two children together. One day he just came home and told her he didn't love her any more and that he wanted a divorce.

'I was devastated,' she tells me. 'I had never felt more unloved, less attractive and sex was absolutely the last thing on my mind.'

She settled back here close to her childhood home of Virginia Water and tried to come to terms with what had happened.

'It was such a shock that it really did take about six months for it to sink in. Then I started to feel slightly better, to emerge from the fog that had been surrounding me.'

It was at that time that she started noticing that one of her colleagues, a man in his early thirties, was paying her a lot of attention.

'At first I thought it was my imagination,' she says. 'But when after a few weeks he asked me out for a drink I realised it wasn't. Then I thought I should say no. I mean it's ridiculous isn't it? A middle-aged woman and a younger man, it's such a cliché. But as a friend of mine pointed out, a cliché is only a cliché because there is some truth in it. And why not have some fun?'

Elizabeth (not her real name) went for the drink and ended up sleeping with her young colleague that same evening.

'We went back to his flat and had sex on his stairs, then his bedroom, then his shower. I felt about 18 again. And I swear to God after that and throughout our liaison my face changed, my posture changed, I looked like a woman who was having good sex, I looked younger.'

Elizabeth is sure that she looked a lot better in part because of all the exercise she was getting. 'I was moving more than I had done for years,' she says. 'And it was addictive, not just the sex, which was great, but that feeling of physical movement and getting fitter and leaner. Added to which of course I was motivated to stay in shape because I cared what I looked like naked.'

She also thinks that part of the reason she looked younger was that she felt more confident. 'I think as we age we lose confidence, we sort of shrink into ourselves. When I was having exciting and great sex with Paul I felt like shouting about it from the rooftops! Somebody wanted me, it was such a fabulous sensation, especially after the rejection I had been through.'

According to research carried out by Dr David Weeks from the Royal Edinburgh Hospital regular sex can make you look seven years younger. He puts this down to the release of endorphins during sex. These so-called feel good hormones are also released during exercise and have several benefits including stimulating the release of human growth hormone, which in turn increases the skin's elasticity and improves bone density, which suffers as we age. Dr Mehmet Oz, a celebrity surgeon known as Dr Oz, concludes that if you have more than 200 orgasms a year you can reduce your physiological age by six years.

Elizabeth agrees with this. 'I walked around with a permanent grin on my face. I was like the cat that got the cream. I felt attractive and lusted after. I can't think of anything more anti-ageing than that.'

After nine months her relationship with Paul ended. There was no acrimony. It just fizzled out.

'It had run its course,' says Elizabeth. 'But now if I'm ever feeling dowdy or old or lacking in confidence I think back to those early days and I feel my face lightening up again. Who knows, I might find another Paul one day, but for now I'm grateful for what he gave me at a very difficult time in my life. And I still stay in shape, because you never know what's around the corner.'

The Clarkson effect

Jeremy Clarkson has talked about how out of shape he is and how his doctors have told him he needs to get fitter. He admits he has 'let himself go'. He is in his fifties and looks pregnant. No, actually he looks worse than that. He looks like an ageing man who has eaten and drunk exactly what he wants and is too lazy to do any exercise. His belly has taken on a life of its own. It's disgusting.

I have found the Clarkson effect is fairly prevalent among my friends' husbands. While my girlfriends work hard to stay in shape, their husbands seem to have decided that for them the war is over. This is not the way to go lads. You don't have to be a metrosexual nowadays to take care of yourself. Even if you don't care what you look like (and actually even if you don't, we do) you must care about how healthy you are, how long (and well) you are going to live?

Clarkson clearly does not. Or maybe he's so arrogant he thinks ill health won't happen to him. But if I were his wife, I'd send him to a boot camp.

To all the pot-bellied blokes out there, it's not that difficult to retain the body you once had. Look at Mick Jagger. Not an ounce of fat on him and the man is 71 years old.

www.triumphfitness.co.uk

The benefits of yoga

I am a middle-aged woman who drinks rather a lot of wine, smokes half a dozen cigarettes a day, and carries an unnecessary amount of weight round her middle.

So far, so ordinary. However, I also stand on my head unsupported in the middle of a room most days.

I resisted doing yoga for the longest time, associating it either with skinny celebrities decked out in Sweaty Betty tank-tops toting Gucci mats, or hippy airheads who liked chanting on the beach.

But then I turned 50. With this milestone came emotional instability and physical fatigue.

At 50, I developed a morbid fear of ageing — specifically of ageing badly — and death.

I couldn't control death, but there was surely something to be done to reduce my chances of being bent double with a stick, of being too tired to go out, too weak to travel, too dependent on others?

Yoga didn't immediately present itself as a solution. I tried a couple of classes in village halls and was discouraged by the fact that I could no longer touch my toes, that my breathing was shallow and ragged when I exerted myself and that my back felt as stiff as a board.

It was an appalling effort just to raise my arms in the air, and standing on one leg was obviously out of the question.

In fact, it wasn't until 2007, when my cousin asked me to accompany her to a yoga sanctuary in India, that I started to take it at all seriously.

The yoga that we did every day at dawn was gentle and structured. The stretching out slowly became enjoyable rather than a chore. My persistent backache was massaged and eased by the twists we did, and my dusty old muscles started to respond. It was both stimulating and relaxing.

I got better at it and therefore wanted to do more of it — and that, of course, is the key. All right, it helped that we were in India, that it was warm, that we were eating delicious vegetarian food and not drinking alcohol. It helped that we didn't have to do the school run, go to a meeting or cook breakfast.

I admit these were ideal circumstances, but the experience gave me the motivation to explore yoga further when I got home.

I have the kind of obsessive personality combined with journalistic scepticism that dictates I won't do anything until I've researched it, approved it and told everyone what I'm about to do.

So it was with yoga. I needed to know what the fuss was all about and whether you could really transform your life.

Here's what I found: scientifically and medically, most of the claims made for yoga practice stand up.

The benefits on both body and mind are legion. The anti-ageing impact is profound.

Doing yoga reduces back pain, improves balance and muscle strength and reverses muscle loss. It improves symptoms of rheumatoid arthritis, menopausal symptoms, even the control of type 2 diabetes.

It decreases anxiety and depression. It hugely enhances flexibility. There are endless sound academic sources to back up these statements as well as the testimony of countless practitioners.

In 1990, headlines were made when a San Francisco cardiologist, Dr Dean Ornish, showed that heart disease can be reversed through yoga combined with dietary changes.

To the astonishment of the medical establishment, he proved that advanced heart patients could actually shrink the fatty plaque deposits that were progressively blocking their coronary arteries.

Instead of taking the conventional route of drugs and surgery, Ornish's study group used simple yoga exercises, meditation and a low cholesterol diet.

His study, The Lifestyle Heart Trial, published in The Lancet, is often cited because mainstream medicine had never before acknowledged that heart disease could be reversed once it had started.

And it's not just heart disease. One of the most interesting books I read which finally convinced me of the miracle of yoga was Yoga As Medicine by a U.S. doctor, Timothy McCall.

Like many, Dr McCall came to yoga in middle age and found it 'incredibly challenging'. He persevered and, astonished by the changes yoga wrought in his own body — and mental state — he began investigating its use for people suffering from a variety of medical conditions, from stress to degenerative arthritis.

It is worth quoting this passage from the book: 'As someone who had been an MD for more than 20 years, I can tell you that yoga is quite simply the most powerful system of overall health and wellbeing I have ever seen.'

By now I was convinced. What's more, I began to realise that although the ancient practice of yoga seems to have been hijacked by impossibly beautiful, thin and hip fashionistas, as well as new age nuts, it is actually for everyone.

There is no one who would not benefit from hoicking themselves off the sofa and stretching out in yoga poses on the rug.

In fact, I would go so far as to say the more you don't think you could do it or need it, the more you should try it.

Different people swear by different styles, but for the beginner the best, most common is gentle Hatha yoga in which you are introduced to the basic yoga poses known as 'asanas'.

There is no leaping about as there is in the fast-paced aerobic Ashtanga Yoga. And you don't risk heart failure by practising in a very hot room (over 100 degrees) — a method pioneered by Bikram Choudhury and beloved by the energetic.

I had the good fortune to find a yoga class that suited me locally and it was a revelation. At first, I was horrified and frustrated by my inability to do what others in the class could do — some in their 70s. I'd been good at gym at school, but the wholesale neglect of my body since I was about 12 became swiftly evident.

After a few weeks, though, I improved dramatically. My 'muscle memory' returned: my body appeared to recall what it's supposed to be able to do.

I learned that I could use the way I breathed to help me move into the poses more easily (learning to breathe properly is central to yoga philosophy) and my confidence rose.

I even became quite cocky, looking around the class when we tried the downward dog position — where your body makes an inverted V with your hands and feet on the floor — to see if my ankles were closer to the ground than anyone else's (for which I was rightly reprimanded by the instructor: 'It's not a competition, Carla!').

It felt so good to be stretched out. My back, in particular, was grateful. Yogis believe that you are as young as your spine is flexible and my spine had evidently been crying out for some exercise. I could hardly wait to lie on my back and swing my legs over to each side to release the tension.

I soon realised this was the most anti-ageing thing I had ever done. All the asanas are based on a sound knowledge of human anatomy and physiology.

By placing the body in certain positions, specific nerves, organs and glands are stimulated. These propel freshly oxygenated blood to flow more freely, relieving joint pain and removing toxins from the internal organs.

Inverted postures such as downward dog, shoulder stand and headstand are especially beneficial — causing blood to stimulate the all-important thyroid gland and boost the immune system.

I was so overjoyed to find an exercise class that didn't bore me rigid that I made a list of all the things I'd learned to do in yoga: stretch every single muscle; take my own body weight on my hands; balance (crucial for oldies); breathe properly through my nose; sit up and stand up straight; remember how to relax (the relaxation period at the end of each session is heaven).

When the body works properly, the mind follows, and now my unquiet mind monkeys around much less. My insomnia has eased. The only downside? I turned into a yoga bore, telling everyone I met that they had to take it up. The only way I could keep my friends was to write a book called *The Reluctant Yogi*. Now they will all speak to me again, unafraid I might turn into some crazed person, and they just point at the book if I so much as use the word yoga.

Despite calling myself a committed convert, there are still some aspects of yoga and the yoga industry that I take issue with. The first is the whole 'spiritual' side of the discipline. I am uncomfortable with the happy-clappy, touchy-feely, new age industry that has grown up around yoga.

Teachers will often tell you that practice is a journey towards self-realisation and the physical discipline is just a tiny part of it.

They implore you to 'feel the divine cosmic energy', to 'connect' with your 'third eye' and 'focus on your chakras'.

Now I know the chakra is a concept that is part of many spiritual traditions — the idea is that they are the energy centres around our bodies, and come in seven colours — but they don't actually exist.

It annoys the heck out of me when yoga teachers mention them in the same way as your hamstring muscles.

Yoga websites are full of online shops selling scented candles and meditation cushions stuffed with organic buckwheat alongside a whole heap of other twaddle — horoscopes and crystals, for example.

This 'widespread mystical schlock' — as one U.S. journalist describes it — is as off-putting as the shameless commercialisation of the multi-million-pound yoga industry.

One in ten Americans now practises yoga — a percentage that is growing year on year. Merchandise such as high-end yoga apparel has become big business, and it's ironic that many yogis see no contradiction between attaining spiritual nirvana and the ringing of earthly cash registers.

Yoga teachers and self-styled gurus such as Bikram Choudury — who created the idea of yoga in overheated studios and claims to be a combination of Elvis and Jesus — have turned themselves into 'brands' and made a fortune.

Even the gloriously rebellious Tara Stiles, the coolest yoga teacher in New York, whose devotees include Jane Fonda and alternative medicine guru Deepak Chopra, has built a profitable empire out of rejecting every spiritual aspect of yoga and concentrating on the body beautiful.

But she talks sense. 'People need yoga, not another religious leader,' she says. Her point is that yoga should not be an elitist cult for the few. It's for everyone. Try it and see.

by Carla McKay

12

Health-spans

'Most people think that ageing is irreversible, but we know there are mechanisms that allow for the reversal of ageing through the correction of diet.'

Deepak Chopra

Off the southern tip of Japan is an island called Okinawa. The culture of this people dictates that they should always leave something on their plate (around a fifth), and always leave the table slightly hungry. As a result, they consume around 60 per cent of the average daily calories in the West.

Okinawa has got the highest proportion of centenarians in the world. They also have 50 per cent less breast and colon cancer than we do, as well as 75 per cent less prostate cancer. They are also 80 per cent more likely than we are to retain their cognitive abilities into old age. And according to Janet Lord, the professor at Birmingham University who specialises in ageing, it's all because they eat less.

'What these people are doing is natural calorie restriction. We have done experiments with animals and it works from the fruit fly up to monkeys where we reduce their normal calorific intake by 25 per cent. The result is two-fold. They live 25 per cent longer, but the key thing is they are healthier.'

Professor Lord explains that the reason eating less has such a positive effect on us dates back to when we were hunter-gatherers. 'It stimulates repair processes in the body. Back in those days we had to repair our own bodies if we were hurt while hunting, and caloric restriction triggers that repair response that actually starts to recycle parts of the body, it's part of our survival instinct.'

Back in today's world there is a diet that emulates this pretty well, called the 5:2 diet. The idea is that you eat normally for five days of the week and for the other two you restrict your calories to less than 500 a day for women and 600 a day for men. Simply put intermittent fasting mimics the environment in which we were shaped when we didn't have three meals a day. And our bodies thrive on it.

The creator of the diet, Dr Michael Mosley, is a journalist and medic who once weighed 14 stone, too much for a man of only 5 foot 11 inches. He tried various diets but none of them worked. Then he started to explore the science behind fasting. He was particularly interested in evidence that fasting reduced your chances of developing diabetes and dementia, both of which his father had suffered from. He started fasting two days a week. In five weeks he lost a stone, his blood sugar fell from close to developing diabetes levels to normal and his fat percentage dropped from 28 to 21 per cent. As if all that wasn't enough, a blood protein called IGF that can predict cancer risk had fallen from high to low. As he says in his book *The Fast Diet*: 'Intermittent fasting can put us back in touch with our human selves. It is a route not only to weight loss, but also to long-term health and wellbeing.'

Professor Lord fasts one day a week, a habit she picked up from an American aunt when she was on her gap year. 'I used to call it my detox day,' she says. 'I only have water for the whole day. You'd think you would be tired by the end of the day, but you're not, in fact it's the opposite, you're completely hyper. Sometimes I get sick of it and stop, but then I always go back to it, I feel much better on it.'

I have tried fasting and you will find my diary of a day's fast below. It's one of those things that you think you can't do if you have to go to work, or look after the children or whatever. So in the end you never do it. But actually people do. When I did my one-day fast my skin was clearer than it has ever been, even after countless expensive facials, and the whites of my eyes literally shone. The following day I didn't gorge myself at all, in fact I wanted to eat less than normal. For days afterwards I was much healthier and abstemious than I had been before the fast. For example, I only had one glass of wine instead of several, only one crumpet for tea not two. I craved healthy foods like curly kale and couldn't imagine ever eating anything processed again. It was a remarkably fast transition and I would highly recommend it. Sadly for me it came just before Christmas so I lost my way slightly, but it's definitely something I will try to kick-start again and keep doing. And even if I don't do the full fast I am definitely going to adopt the 5:2 diet, which of course will seem like a doddle when compared with not eating at all! I really believe calorie restriction is the way forward, but I don't want to do it every day. The 5:2 diet apparently gives you all the benefits of calorie restriction but you only have the pain two days a week. And actually looking at some of the recipes in the book, it doesn't even look that painful.

So remember when it comes to eating, less is more. As the Irish celebrity hairdresser Robert Chambers put it when I sat next to him at a dinner party (which rather put me off my food: his words not Robert himself!); 'It's not what we eat that makes us feel well, it's what we don't eat.'

When we're not fasting, it's important to eat properly. 'The most important thing for ageing well is diet and what you put into your body,' says Claudia Louch, who runs the Claudia Louch Natural Skin Clinic in Harley Street. 'A healthy balanced diet is not just essential for a well-functioning body, it also vastly contributes to healthy, balanced skin.'

Claudia is the kind of formidable German that makes you slightly nervous. She is an attractive blonde woman with a list of letters after her name that make you feel incredibly inferior. Her main interest is in human nutrition and how it affects us.

'Healthy skin starts from the inside out,' continues Claudia. 'And it is possible to make drastic improvements in your skin by modifying your daily diet to make sure it includes the optimum amount of vitamins and minerals.'

There are certain things we should avoid; processed foods being one of them. 'Don't even buy vegetables ready chopped,' she says. 'I know it's convenient, but the moment you actually break up a fruit or a vegetable the vitamin C evaporates.'

Sugar is another thing we should avoid. Claudia doesn't even talk about cakes and biscuits, it is a given that we would not do that to ourselves. It is well known that sugar is damaging, it eats away at our collagen causing inflammation and wrinkles. In fact, I met a man recently who has completely given up sugar; he was quite dull, but his skin looked fabulous. But back to Claudia; she says we must under no circumstances drink fruit juice, or even give fruit juice to our children. 'It is full of sugar, just think about it, one glass of apple juice takes ten apples to make. That's a lot of sugar, added to which you would never eat ten apples in one day.' She does however suggest we eat an apple a day. 'It contains the perfect amount of Vitamin C we need.'

Interestingly she is not in favour of vegetarianism or a vegan diet. 'You need a good mixture of protein, vegetables and carbohydrates,' says Claudia. 'The vegetarian or vegan diet is often not the best because you get a lot of sugar from that diet.'

Claudia advocates 'eating like a farmer', by which she means 'eat what is around you, eat good seasonal local food, not something imported. And when it comes to meat and fish, go organic.'

Here is Claudia's list of nutrients that make your skin glow:

* Vitamins C and E are both antioxidants that help reduce free radical damage of collagen and elastin. But don't take Vitamin C supplements. The lowest dose available is still at least 12 times more than our bodies can absorb so our kidneys then have to work hard to get rid of it. So again just eat an apple a day.
* Purified vegetable oils and fish oils (Omega 3 fatty acids) contain mono apha hydroxy acids (AHAs) that help reduce inflammation.
* Beta-carotene, which is found in carrots and other carotenoids such as tomatoes help protect from UV rays.
* Selenium, which is found in wheat germ, brazil nuts, eggs and brown rice, is an antioxidant mineral that aids skin tissue elasticity.
* Resveratrol (found in grapes and red wine) is an antioxidant so helps the fight against free radicals and has also been found to prevent skin cancer.

Resveratrol has long been touted as a miracle ingredient when it comes to anti-ageing, which is fabulous for us red wine drinkers. Unfortunately there is no longer a reason to down bottles of red wine to get our fix, it's readily available in skin care products. You can't walk down the King's Road in London without being accosted by someone selling a product called Vine Vera. The line was established in the US and moved to London next. Their sales technique is rather off-putting, as sales assistants literally pounce on you as you walk past and practically drag you into the shop to show you the immediate and miraculous effects on their creams. A salesperson puts the cream on one eye and then compares it to the other eye. Obviously the one with cream on looks more plumped up and healthier.

I fell for the spiel of course and ended up buying the eye cream for a 50 per cent discount, or so I was told. Buying the cream entitled me to a free facial, which is when I met Yasmin Bensalem, a facial therapist for Vine Vera, who did slightly restore my faith in the company. Yasmin agrees with me that the sales technique was pushy but insists the product is good. 'The antioxidant potential of resveratrol has been shown to be greater than both vitamins E and C,' she tells me as I lie in the basement of their King's Road shop on a black faux fur blanket that reminded me of something out of *50 Shades of Grey.* 'It has been scientifically proven to delay the ageing process. And we use other natural antioxidants in our range, such as green tea extracts, omega 3 fish oil and caviar and olive oil extracts.' The eye cream is fine, I have the serum and the moisturiser, it slides on well and the effect is nice. I wonder if it contains something that gives my skin a slight glow as it seems to sparkle a little after I put it on, and I'm not daft enough to believe that is the effect of the resveratrol, however gullible I might have been to fall for the sales patter.

There is always some new diet, or some new piece of advice telling us what we should and shouldn't eat. Suddenly something we have been happily eating for decades is found to be terribly dangerous. Or we are told that yes we should eat fish, but not too much, due to the mercury content. This is why I like the 5:2 diet, it just seems to make such good sense. I am also a great believer in the Viva Mayr way of eating (and living). Viva Mayr is an exclusive Austrian clinic run by a wonderful couple called Harald and Christina Stossier. With them it is more about how you eat than what you eat. For example, you have to chew, and chew a lot. This works well on so many levels. If you do chew each mouthful the recommended 30 times not only will your body be more able to absorb the nutrients of what you are chewing, and your digestive system have less work to do, but your brain will receive a signal saying you have eaten enough. It's a win-win situation. You should be aware of every single mouthful you take. Chew without holding your cutlery, it will slow you down. And going back to the calorie restriction idea, train yourself to stop when you've had enough, or in fact before you've had enough. The generation during the Second World War was told to eat what was on their plate. In some cultures they don't know when they will eat next. But in our situation we always have enough, even more than enough; we have to change our habits and realise that not finishing everything on our plate can be a good thing. We have to stop when we feel we've had enough. Even slightly before. If you eat slowly and chew well you will know when it is enough. It is very difficult to describe the feeling of enough as it is different for everyone. One thing is for sure; when a button pops off your jeans it's too much.

Try to recognise the difference between hunger and a tendency to eat, craving for food because you see it, rather than because you are truly hungry.

Try to train yourself by eating just a piece of bread with a cup of vegetable soup, that may not sound like a substantial meal but if you chew it extensively and take the soup with a small spoon, you will soon have that absolutely enough feeling. It takes a minimum of a few days of eating less to get a feeling of an optimal amount that leaves you satisfied.

If you feel tired after a meal you have eaten too much or you have eaten the wrong thing. You can safely skip dinner now and again and you won't die of starvation during the night, I promise! As Professor Lord says, you get more energy from eating less.

One thing I have not yet touched on in this chapter is obesity. A recent study carried out by scientists in Canada concludes that obesity may (and often will) mean you have around 20 less healthy years at the end of your life than your slimmer peers. It is also likely to mean you die up to eight years before they do, depending on just how overweight you are. Being overweight is one of the most damaging things you can do to yourself. The scariest statistic is that the younger you have weight issues, the more detrimental it is to your good health in later life. And this is particularly worrying when you take into account that one in ten children are obese when they start school aged five. By the time they leave primary school at 11 this has risen to one in five. What a life sentence we are passing on to them. As Maureen Talbot, Senior Cardiac Nurse at the British Heart Foundation says about the Canadian study: 'The study demonstrates that if you're overweight at a younger age, the impact on your health is much greater. Both in life expectancy and in the years of life free from chronic diseases.'

So staying slim when young is like an insurance policy for when you or your children are older. It is certainly in my top five things to do to stay young along with a good diet, using sunscreen, exercising, and not smoking.

Top Hydration Tip

Every time you are offered something to drink, be it at the hairdresser's or at a meeting ask for water. None of us drink enough water and it is essential for ageing well. By asking for coffee or tea you are potentially drinking something that's damaging you. Water will benefit you. And when you drink alcohol, try to balance out the intake with a glass or two of water between each glass of wine or whatever it is you're drinking.

Fat freezing

What I tried: The Sculpt Cryo 4, a revolutionary system to eliminate stubborn areas of fat. Cryolipolysis is the latest and most powerful way to remove fat with permanent results. It can remove up to 26 per cent of fatty tissues in one treatment making it the equivalent of a non-invasive liposuction.

What I expected: I had heard a lot about this machine from my beautician. She called it everything from incredible to painless to nothing short of miraculous. The way it works is that it heats up your fat cells causing them to come to the surface of your skin. Then it freezes them. Which kills them. And you spend the next six weeks eliminating them from your body. A machine that can take away your fat with no pain and no side effects in just one session? What's not to like?

What happened: My therapist took some before pictures of me, urging me to let it all hang out. It's amazing how one naturally holds one's stomach in when a camera appears. I did my best to oblige. Then I was told to lie down and she spread a cloth that was wet with some gel-like substance on my stomach. 'You have to have this,' she told me. 'Otherwise you'll get frostbite.' The idea of frostbite did make me slightly nervous, but I stayed put. She then manoeuvred a contraption over my stomach and warned me that it would feel a bit like a very strong hoover sucking up my belly. She was right, my belly was soon engulfed into the oblong shaped head of the machine and I lay there a bit like a beetle who has landed on its back, unable to move. The sight of my flesh being pummelled was quite disgusting and I was relieved that I would soon be rid of it. The process wasn't painful, although you couldn't really call it comfortable either. I felt heat then cold. This went on for about half an hour until the machine finally released me and I was able to breathe properly once more.

Wrinkles or wrinkle free? It will take six weeks for the full results to show but already after two weeks I can see there is a difference. My stomach looks more toned. I am looking forward to the full effect of joining the 'fat-freezing revolution' as my beautician calls it. Definitely a beauty. Although you'd have to say the machine itself is a beast.

Star Product

What: teapigs, organic matcha

Why: Anything that has been drunk by Buddhist monks for over 900 years has got to be a good thing. Matcha is one of those buzzwords I kept hearing during my anti-ageing quest and it stressed me out that I hadn't got onto it. Finally I found a little box of the magic formula. The claims are pretty impressive; it contains 137 times the antioxidants of green tea, it is energising due to the combination of theophylline and L-theanine, which give our bodies an energy boost. At the same time, it is calming. Apparently L-theanine stimulates our alpha brain waves, creating a state of mental alertness and focus. After two weeks 60 per cent of people who took part in a trial said they noticed an improvement in skin, hair and nails. Most impressively a friend of mine told me she had to stop drinking it because she lost so much weight. I find the thought of 137 times the antioxidants of green tea whizzing around my body slightly disconcerting, but I have become a matcha addict. It really does boost your energy, and you also have that smug feeling of drinking something that is actually doing you some good as opposed to a latte or a cup of English Breakfast tea. It is pricey but I find you can refill your cup endless times and it still looks as green as it did to begin with.

Beauty food

A few years ago I visited a friend who was living in the genteel English city of Bath. We had lunch together with her four-year-old daughter.

I was amazed to see the little girl tucking into carrots, blueberries, broccoli and even spinach. I can't get my children to eat anything that is remotely healthy and if it is green, forget it.

'How do you do it?' I asked her.

'I tell her it's "beauty food",' she replied. 'Works every time.'

Beauty food is food that makes you beautiful. As opposed to food that does nothing but fill a need (emotional or otherwise) such as a doughnut. Garlic, for example, may not help you to make friends, but it is good for reducing wrinkles. It apparently restores skin tissue.

And instead of buying expensive creams containing Retin

A you can munch on carrots, which do the same job of protecting the outer layer of your skin.

Creams with collagen in them are a waste of money; collagen cannot be absorbed topically. You need to ingest it (or inject it). So eat lots of citrus fruits or drink lots of citrus drinks because citrus fruits form collagen. If you're after smoother skin then bake a sweet potato or two. These spuds are extremely high in vitamin A so are a great source of skin food.

If you suffer from spots then you should try some wheatgerm. Add it to your hot chocolate, cereal, yoghurt, whatever you like. It's a miracle worker.

The anti-ageing expert Dr Nicholas Perricone has long advocated eating things that are antioxidant and anti-inflammatory. 'Antioxidants can impede and even repair the damage to skin cells that come with aging,' Perricone writes in his book *The Wrinkle Cure*. 'Soft, radiant, younger-looking skin is the gratifying result.'

He suggests we live off foods such as blueberries (great if you live in Scandinavia or Canada but rather expensive in the rest of the world) and wild salmon, which is rich in omega-3 essential fatty acids. Omega-3s help to keep skin young, supple and radiant. Wild salmon also contains astaxanthin, a powerful antioxidant and anti-inflammatory. If you're not a fish person then nuts are a good substitute, especially almonds and walnuts. He also advocates eating leafy greens, asparagus and at least an apple a day.

If you're feeling ambitious (or desperate) you can try his wild salmon diet. You eat just that for a couple of weeks. Friends of mine have tried it and swear they looked 10 years younger, although they never want to see another salmon, wild or otherwise.

Bring on the beauty food, I'm convinced. Now I just need to convince my children.

A Fishy Face Mask

What I tried: The Salmon Facial

What I expected: Dermatologist Dr Nicholas Perricone says we should all eat nothing but salmon for weeks and that our skin would look ten years younger. I really don't like eating salmon so figured I could try plastering it on my skin instead when I heard about the salmon mask.

What happened: My therapist explained that the salmon mask is a revolutionary deluxe innovation developed from Salmon Egg extract, which is rich in essential amino acids and peptides and increases the natural collagen in your skin. She began by cleansing and then massaged off any dead skin. For most of the treatment I was under the salmon mask, a kind of death mask they call a gypsy mask, that dries in the form of your face. My therapist asked me if I wanted to take it home, but I decided against it. It is under this mask that the salmon facial works its magic, rejuvenating and thoroughly nourishing you skin.

Wrinkles or wrinkle free? My therapist suggested I do this treatment six times in one week for optimum results, but I felt that was slight overkill, especially as my husband told me he would slap me with a real salmon if I tried to go for six beauty treatments in one week. My skin felt really moisturised and nourished afterwards, and was truly glowing, an effect that lasted for days.

The One-Day-Fast diary

I decided to fast on one of the rare occasions I was alone with no husband and no children. Here is a diary of how the day went…

5.30am Wake up, already hungry.

6.30 Still trying to ignore hunger pangs and go back to sleep. The plan is to sleep to midday if possible so as not to feel hungry all day.

9.30 Managed to get back to sleep in fitful bursts. Now have to concede defeat and get up to face the day without food.

9.40 Try to change attitude and look on fasting day as a gift. Get into yoga kit.

9.50 What if I faint doing yoga due to lack of food and hit head on the kitchen table? It could be days before I am found. I suppose upside will be I have fasted unconsciously.

10.00 Make myself a hot water and ginger. Hunger pangs ferocious. Must stop thinking about food.

10.30 It's amazing how much time you spend planning what to eat every day, shopping and cooking. Not to mention eating. Have a feeling I will get a lot done with no food to deal with. And that the day will seem very long indeed…

10.35 It's still morning.

11.15 Did yoga, felt very pure. Then very hungry. One upside though to fasting is you don't have to worry about your food settling before you exercise.

Noon Just licked an envelope, no, not as a lunch substitute but to close it. Tasted hideous, my taste buds are clearly sensitized already.

12.30 Feeling light-headed.

12.45 Working seems very tough. My mind keeps

wandering. Towards the fridge.

1.00   Have now done more than 12 hours if you count the time after dinner last night and sleeping. Surely that's a day?

1.30   My friend Carla helpfully pops by to tell me how much she's already eaten today.

2.00   Starting really to crave food, but funnily enough not things like chocolate but raw food.

3.00   A cup of Detox Tea to stave off the hunger pangs. Tastes great. Amazing.

3.30   Maybe if I just eat one carrot?

3.45   But I've come this far. Have to make it until bedtime.

4.00   Now feeling seriously lightheaded. Typing as if I'm drunk.

4.30   I wish that apple would stop staring at me.

4.45   I keep thinking I feel odd, then realise it's just hunger.

5.00   This must be the longest I haven't eaten for, well, decades. Feels like the longest day.

5.15   Am reading the 5:2 diet book for inspiration.

5.30   Still very hungry. Really about to pounce on that apple.

6.00   Am going to have a bath to try to stave off apple molestation.

6.30   Am wondering if I can have a glass of wine.

6.45   Another Detox Tea. Actually feeling less hungry, think the worst might be over.

7.00   Watching Breaking Bad. Definitely good for taking one's mind off food.

7.30   Oh no Jesse is eating waffles.

8.00   Almost there, suddenly feel elated. Planning breakfast.

9.30   Head to bed and read, stomach quieter. Fall asleep easily.

3.30am Wake up and can't understand why I'm not hungry. Fall back to sleep within seconds.

7.30   Wake and survey the results. Skin clear, eyes clear. Head extremely clear. Time for breakfast!

13

French attitudes

'Life shrinks or expands in proportion to one's courage.'
Anaïs Nin

There is an expression to describe French women when they're really perfect French to the tips of their nails. This means that everything is just right. The hairstyle is flattering, the clothes are stylish, the make-up is not overbearing and the nails, of course, are manicured.

And this attention to detail does not diminish with age. If anything it gets worse, or better, depending on how you want to look at it. There is not one millimetre of her body that a French woman ignores or neglects. If you're going to follow the French way of ageing then you probably need to set aside a little more time for your beauty regime than you have been. You don't leave the house until you're groomed to perfection; nothing is ignored. And a top French beautician also told me that sleeping with your make-up on for just one night ages your skin by eight days. *Quelle horreur!*

Sexiness for French women does not diminish with age. I remember when I was doing interviews in Galeries Lafayette in Paris. I picked random women to talk to about whether they always wore matching underwear ('Is there any other kind?', was the response) and other important issues relating to their lingerie habits. I spotted a woman who must have been in her mid-sixties looking at some very slinky black underwear. I asked her what sort of underwear she normally bought. 'Sexy underwear,' she replied. 'It has to be pretty and sexy, I want to look good when I undress.' Her hair was grey, but well cut in a bob, her clothes elegant and her manner confident. In France a woman is never unattractive because she is old.

Maybe French women aren't daunted by age in part because they have such good modern role models. Look at Catherine Deneuve, Inés de la Fressange and the actress Isabelle Huppert. Even their politicians age well, for example Ségolène Royale who when I interviewed her was carrying her lip-gloss.

The actress Charlotte Rampling is over 60. She has been labelled the thinking man's crumpet and is still incredibly sexy. She lives in France and has adopted a French attitude towards ageing. She has not had plastic surgery and is not considering it. 'Many women are destroying their faces trying to look young,' she says in an interview with the *Sunday Times*. 'Ageing can make you quite beautiful. A few wrinkles here and there but so what?'

Nor is age a barrier to seduction if you're French. Their history is littered with popular stories. Colette, the writer, was famous for having a string of young lovers who found her irresistible, even in her old age. She was dancing on tables well into her sixties. One of her most popular books, *Chéri*, is all about a young man's love for an older woman. In it, the heroine Léa devotes herself to the amorous education of the beautiful young Chéri. When the time comes for Chéri to marry, he finds it impossible to leave her. Aged 49, she holds more allure for him than his young wife. 'Everyone knows,'

Léa would say, 'that a well-made body lasts a long time.' French men like older women. Balzac had many lovers and almost every one of them was older than him. 'Our young girls are too concerned with making a rich match, passion comes later,' he said.

Diane de Poitiers, Duchess of Valentinois (1490-1566), was 18 years older than her lover King Henri II, but he much preferred her to his wife Catherine de Medici. In fact, his wife had trouble conceiving an heir and Diane, realising that an annulment of the marriage and a new queen could compromise her position, used to arouse Henri before sending him to his wife's bed to complete the task. His dynastic duty done he would return to Diane's bed. Catherine eventually became pregnant and bore the king a healthy son. Catherine de Medici couldn't understand her husband's obsession with his ageing mistress and so had a carpenter drill two holes on the floor directly above Diane's bedroom. She and her maid would watch them making love and conceded, weeping, that he 'had never used me so well'.

Diane was one of the first examples of a woman ageing (astonishingly) attractively. She always looked after herself, she ate mainly fruit, nuts and vegetables. She was convinced ice cold baths retained her radiant complexion and energy. She also exercised regularly, slept sitting up to reduced wrinkles and wore a velvet mask while outside to protect her skin. Her regular beauty habits paid off, she was stunning until the day she died. All that sounds tempting, I admit, but mad.

French women see beauty as something to work on. They don't ever take it for granted. They start at a young age by protecting their skin from the sun and eating well. 'We see regular and healthy habits as far more effective than layers of concealing make-up,' says my French friend Nadine.

Jeanette who is from Yorkshire but has lived in Montpellier

for almost 15 years says she is encouraged by the French attitude towards age. 'Back home friends of mine would start to look old as soon as they had children,' she says. 'Here you see people with grandchildren and they still look sexy. They have this ageing thing sussed. They continue to take pride in their appearance, they look polished.'

So it's back to the beauty regime and looking after yourself. Grooming of course is key. Especially as you get older, as there is much more need for it. But the French philosophy is very much that if you are going to age gracefully you need to start young. You need to invest in creams and exfoliating potions, eat well and exercise. Once you have the basics you need to adapt your look with your age so that you always look natural. This will mean lighter hair as you get older and less make-up. You will also have to stay thin. But I don't think you need to be boring.

'You should always follow fashion a bit,' says Inés de la Fressange, who was born in 1957 but looks about 25. 'But don't forget your own style. Take some risks, go to some new shops, new places, get ideas from magazines. But above all don't wander around thinking young people are all terrible and talking about the past all the time. Hang out with young people. Appreciate them. Also appreciate your life with the wisdom that comes with age. If you decide that your life is not so bad and you're actually quite lucky then it becomes a reality. You can go out and hate everybody and hate all the other cars on the road but it will show; you have the face you deserve.'

There is a lot more pressure now on women to look young. A woman of 50 today is not viewed the same way she was 20 years ago, when she was basically history. Forty is no longer middle aged (thank God). Anyone between 18 and 80 can wear a well-cut pair of jeans, a T-shirt and jacket and look great. There is no mystery to ageing with grace; it is common sense. And for the French plastic surgery is not the answer.

'There is something more honest about growing old gracefully without too much intervention,' says Nadine. 'And of course we don't yet know the full effects of all this invasive stuff people are doing.'

Personally I haven't seen too many bad effects, although a friend of mine who had Botox back when it was first really taking off then had to have eyelid surgery because her eyelids drooped as a result of it.

The lesson from French women is that age is not something that needs to dictate the way we look and are. Their philosophy is elegance and grooming throughout life, with maybe more attention on it as we grow older. Partly because as we grow older we need to pay more attention. Those stray hairs crop up, our nails get more brittle and so forth.

When I first met her, Hermine de Clermont-Tonnerre was the coolest chick there was, a French 'it' girl, who was in her mid twenties, dressed in Dior and with hair streaked a series of different shades, she confidently told me of her plans to be the first grandmother to walk on the moon. 'But I will have to stay hyper rock and roll,' she added.

Gymphobia

French women hate the gym. And they believe in miracle cures to combat fat things and cellulite. Evidence of this can be found in those magical places, French pharmacies, where the shelves are packed full of anti-cellulite creams and body shaping creams. I tried a treatment that is popular in France called the VelaShape II, a machine that can apparently take two centimetres off your thighs, stomach or whatever area you want reduced in just one hour.

'What is your problem?' asked Leticia the therapist lifting up my dress to survey me.

Where to begin…?

I opted to have the tops of my thighs and lower buttocks done. Leticia asked me to lie down on my front. She attached the head of the VelaShape to a long tube. The machine has two metal rollers on it that pummel your skin, the hose acting as a kind of cosmetic hoover. These actions combined with infrared light and radio frequency heat your tissue thus tightening and toning the skin.

It was not an uncomfortable sensation, although a couple of times it got very hot, but otherwise it's a little bit like a massage by a machine, or one of those massage chairs you sit in at the hairdresser's.

The aim of the VelaShape treatment is to improve cellulite and reduce circumference. This can be achieved in just one session, although if you have more the results are obviously more dramatic.

After my VelaShape I was strapped into a sort of moon suit that fills with air and then deflates every few minutes. Called Pressotherapy, this treatment is good for fluid retention and lymphatic flow.

I walked out of the treatment feeling very thin. The results of a heat treatment keep on improving for weeks after your spa visit and my buttocks do still look in fairly good shape. That nasty bit of flesh just at the top of my thighs seems to have reduced. However, as Leticia points out, you can double the effects by exercising and eating well too. These machines are not to be relied on to transform your body unless you're willing to work at it as well. Even if you are French!

Little tips on dressing like a French woman
Wearing matching underwear is one rule a French woman never breaks. Underwear should also make you feel good. Perfect grooming is also about confidence and a seriously sexy set of smalls is going to give you lots of that. What does it matter if no one knows you're wearing red lace underneath your grey suit? As France's leading lingerie designer Chantal Thomass says: 'Women wear underwear for all sorts of reasons, but mainly for themselves.'

To be perfectly groomed, your clothes must of course be impeccable. Ideally they should also be chic and stylish. If you want some tips on how to dress then go to a professional dresser in a department store. This service is normally free. The dresser will talk to you to get an idea of what you're after and then go and choose clothes for you that she thinks will suit you. I did this at Galeries Lafayette in Paris and was amazed when the dresser came back with a purple top. 'This is your colour,' she told me. It is not a colour I would ever have considered before but now I am always on the look-out for a little something in purple. My husband says it's the first sign of a mid-life crisis but I figure there's nothing wrong with growing old colourfully.

Accessories are essential when it comes to the perfectly

groomed look. In fact, the above-mentioned dresser said to me the single most important thing to do was to buy a really good handbag. This will cost you a fortune but can last five years or more. And now that vintage is all the rage, there's no need to change every season. I really love Tod's bags (and shoes for that matter). They are horrifyingly expensive but the style is unmistakably classic and the quality is great.

The same rule applies to shoes. There is that memorable line in *The Silence of the Lambs* when Jodie Foster first meets Hannibal Lecter. 'You know what you look like to me, with your good bag and your cheap shoes?' he says to her. Ever since I heard this, I have doubled my shoe budget.

Then there is the French woman's secret weapon; the scarf. French women seem to instinctively know how to tie a scarf; I have watched them. The trick is to start from the front and then bring it back round before knotting it at the side, or at the front. And avoid strangling yourself at the same time. In fact when I first moved to France I really felt like strangling the chic women that live here. But it's easier to copy them.

Top French Tips to Age Attractively

* Even if you don't have time for a manicure, make sure your nails are clean and covered in clear polish.
* Always remember Coco Chanel's quote 'Elegance is refusal'. Don't pile into unnecessary calories.
* Move at every given opportunity; if you're asked to get something from upstairs look upon it as an excuse to tone your thighs.
* Stay mentally groomed; keep up with the news, latest exhibitions and films.
* Always sleep on your back to avoid wrinkles to your

face and décolletage.

* Don't neglect your feet, make sure they are presentable. It's the attention to detail that sets French women apart.
* Think about your posture, standing straight makes you look better groomed immediately.
* Always carry a natural-coloured lip-gloss, it will make you look and feel better groomed if you have glossy lips.
* Carry a breath freshener or some mints to freshen your mouth.
* Clean your bags and shoes regularly. Nothing lets an outfit down like a pair of scuffed or dirty shoes.
* You need white teeth to be perfectly groomed; use a whitening toothpaste and if you want to splurge get them whitened professionally.

Top Tip

If beauty comes from the inside…

This is a miraculous little gadget that may not have immediately visible results. Dubbed 'your most personal trainer' it is a small device that trains your pelvic floor muscles, a set of muscles that sits like a hammock between your tail bone and your pubic bone. These muscles weaken with, among other things, age and childbirth. The Elvie trains these muscles leading (so it says on the box) to 'better core stability, control and even better sex.' The device itself is a small, smooth oblong green gadget with a tail. You use it with an app that you connect to the device and it tracks your pelvic floor squeezes with a small gem that moves on the screen as you squeeze. The aim is to do at least three times a week and each workout lasts about three to four minutes.

It's elegant, easy to use and effective. I'm a total convert. And an added rather fabulous side effect is that your abs somehow get toned as well. I have noticed a great improvement in mine.

elvie.com or johnlewis.com

14

Silly money

'Ageing can be fun if you lay back and enjoy it.'
Clint Eastwood

Have you ever wondered what it would really be like to have all the money and time in the world to spend on making yourself look younger? Me too. And for a month I got the chance to do just that. I spent four weeks being Trinny Woodall, or rather trying out all the anti-ageing treatments and tips she has so publicly talks about that keep her looking good at 52. I did everything from Botox to full-face threading, vitamin pill popping, face masks and more.

Was it all worth it? Do I look or feel any younger? Read on to find out…

Foreo Luna Silicone Cleansing Brush

I have tried a number of cleansing brushes and after a few goes they all feel a bit grimy. There's no risk of that with this ultra-hygienic silicone device.

On one side there are hundreds of silicone dimples. These vibrate as you move it across your face, apparently unclogging pores of makeup residue, as well as 99.5% of dirt and oil. These dimples also exfoliate dead skin, which means your skin looks brighter and your skincare products are more efficiently absorbed.

The other side of the device is flat with ridges on. According to the blurb, this is the side you use with the 'anti-ageing mode' which 'delivers lower-frequency pulsations that, when applied to wrinkle-prone areas, reduces the visibility of fine lines and wrinkles.'

Trinny swears by it although I haven't yet got to grips with it.

However I do love the cleansing side. My skin looks instantly translucent and sparkling clean. It's as quick and easy to use as a toothbrush. Definitely a keeper.

www.foreo.com

EFFICACY: 4/5 | VALUE FOR MONEY: 4/5

Sisley Black Rose Cream Mask

This is a truly miraculous product. It doesn't matter how hungover you are or how drab your skin looks, pop this on and you look almost instantly refreshed. You don't even need to use that much so it lasts an age. I usually use it first thing if I'm looking a bit ropey, it makes my skin look instantly refreshed and slightly dewy. I leave it on for about ten minutes and if there is any residue take it off with a cotton pad soaked with toner. But more often than not my skin has absorbed it all. If you need more nourishing support then mix it with Sisley's Black Rose Oil and leave overnight — heavenly!

Sisley Black Rose Cream Mask

www.sisley-paris.co.uk

EFFICACY : 4/5 | VALUE FOR MONEY: 3/5

Rudolph Facial Scrub Mask

Trinny uses the exfoliating mask of this Danish brand, which contains granules made from acai berry and apricot to gently cleanse and exfoliate your skin. This is also a mask so the idea is you rub it into damp skin first and then you leave it on for 10 minutes to half an hour to give the organic oils and shea butter time to nourish the skin. It is quite an earthy, unperfumed product, which you would expect from an organic brand, and you do need to make sure you remove all the granules or you'll be rubbing them off for the rest of the day, but the results are good — my skin looked clean and bright afterwards. I now use it two to three times a week.

Rudolph Facial Scrub Mask *www.rudolphcare.dk/en*

EFFICACY : 4/5 | VALUE FOR MONEY: 3/5

Cherry Lip Gel Patch

I have no idea how Trinny found this weird and wonderful product from Korea. It contains cherry extract The idea is that it nourishes, moisturises and plumps up your lips by removing dead skin cells and moisturizing the lips. It is a pleasant smelling jelly-like thin patch in the shape of some oversized lips. You put it on for 15 minutes and lie back looking like a clown. I liked the feel of it, although I wouldn't say the results were dramatic. My lips did look slightly more plumped afterwards although the effect only lasted for a day. So perfect if you're off on a night out.

Etude House Cherry Lip Gel Patch *www.amazon.co.uk*

EFFICACY : 3/5 | VALUE FOR MONEY: 3/5

The Vampire Facial

The Vampire Facial, or to give it its official name the Platelet-rich Plasma (PRP) therapy involves blood and needles, two of my least favourite things. But Trinny swears says it's one of the most effective anti-ageing tools out there.

A nurse takes a small syringe of blood from my arm from which the platelet rich plasma is going to be extracted. This is the substance that is naturally produced by the body to help the healing process when, for example, you cut yourself and it is known in the industry as 'liquid gold' because of its ability to stimulate cell growth and rejuvenate skin. To extract the plasma from the blood the physician uses a centrifuge to isolate the platelet rich plasma from the blood.

While this is happening, one of the nurses covers my face in a topical anaesthetic so when the plasma is reinjected into me, it hurts less.

This is done via a derma-pen, which in itself creates trauma to the skin that encourages collagen and elastin production.

Dr Veil who is carrying out the process recommends three vampire facials over a period of three months and then one a year as a top up.

Afterwards I look like a tomato and I feel like my face is pressed up against a hot fire. I can't wear any make-up for the rest of the day and try to avoid any human contact.

The following day I look like I fell asleep in the sun and while the day after, I look vaguely normal my skin starts to flake off, revealing younger skin underneath. Thankfully this process is quite quick and five days after the treatment I start to see the benefits. My skin is incredibly clear, it looks almost constantly exfoliated and cleansed. And it gets better as the weeks pass.

Dr Veil says he has clients who are totally addicted to it. I'm not sure I will ever become a Vampire Facial addict but it's certainly something I would do again.

www.lcas.com

EFFICACY : 5/5 | VALUE FOR MONEY: 3/5

Full-face threading and eyebrow shaping

Threading is a process by which hairs are removed by trapping them between two twisted pieces of thread and pulling them out. Many people have used the technique to shape their eyebrows but I'd never considered having my entire face threaded. However, the sad fact is that as we age, due to our increased testosterone levels hair sprouts in the most unseemly places. The face is one of them. I didn't even think about the fact that parts of my face was covered in a very light down until it was gone. I can't pretend the treatment was painless; think leg waxing and quadruple it, but the difference is incredible. My face looks more defined, my skin clearer and make-up glides on with ease. I have heard people say that taking out the fuzz can lead to darker hairs growing back but it's too soon to tell

I will most definitely keep going with the threading, a total revelation and I have Trinny to thank for that.

minxbeauty.com

EFFICACY : 5/5 | VALUE FOR MONEY: 3/5

Botox

Botox is an injectable substance that paralyses the muscles that cause the movement that causes wrinkles. It is a quick and fairly painless process. I was in and out of the clinic in less than ten minutes. You basically smile and frown so the dermatologist can see which muscles need to be targeted, they inject you and then for the rest of the day you need to avoid doing anything that might move the Botox to somewhere you don't want it (so don't fall asleep on your face for example or have a facial). The poison (yes that is what it is) takes around three days to work but once it does you will be utterly hooked. In fact tsome recent research concludes that Botox is actually good for our mental health as well as our wrinkles.

It's the single most dramatically effective anti-ageing treatment there is and I love it, but make sure you go to a properly qualified dermatologist, preferably someone whose work you have seen on friends, as done badly it can look truly disastrous.

www.lcas.com

EFFICACY : 5/5 | VALUE FOR MONEY: 5/5

Hair roots, tint and highlights

Good hair is essential to looking young and glossy — Trinny has her roots done every few weeks and colour tweaked — and this was possibly the thing that most dramatically changed my appearance. As we age our complexions are less able to deal with block colour, especially if it's dark. The hairdresser I saw suggested we lighten everything up a tone or two and add some highlights around my face. My hair looks livelier and less dowdy, and when the grey hairs do start to come through between root treatments they will be a lot less obvious next to my new light locks than they were next to my dark brown ones.

www.michaeljohn.co.uk

EFFICACY : 5/5 | VALUE FOR MONEY: 3/5

Laser Facial

Trinny is right about lasers, they really are the future of anti-ageing. Different lasers work in different ways but the Clearlift facial I had uses laser technology delivered to the lower dermis where it tricks the body into thinking that the skin has been wounded and kicks off a healing process. This stimulates growth of new cells and collagen helping to repair sun damaged skin. The results were immediate; my skin looked plumped and incredibly clear. I had no redness or discomfort at all. The following morning the skin above my eyes seemed tighter. There seemed to be some very minimal swelling on the skin at the top of my cheekbones but really there is no downtime to speak of. And as with all collagen stimulating treatments this is just the beginning as they continue to work for weeks after the actual facial.

Clearlift *michaeljohn.co.uk*

EFFICACY : 4/5 | VALUE FOR MONEY: 4/5

Hands, décolletage and neck laser treatment

It's all very well looking after our face, but there are three areas that can give away our age like no other: the hands, décolletage and neck. I tried the Ellipse VL treatment, that uses lasers to boost collagen production, stimulate new cells, soften wrinkles and improve skin tone. It is especially effective on age spots and pigmentation marks. The Ellipse uses light so-called Selective Waveband Technology (SWT). Three different types of wavelengths are used, the first targeting age spots and pigmentation marks, the second stimulates collagen growth and softens lines while the last improve skin elasticity. There is some downtime — pigmentation goes darker initially and may even scab over before the scabs fall off (don't pick them whatever you do!) revealing clearer skin. They recommend three treatments over three months and an annual top up. I saw results, especially on my hands in ten days after just one treatment, and will definitely keep going.

www.skin-matters.co.uk or www.ellipseuk.com

EFFICACY : 4/5 | VALUE FOR MONEY: 3/5

Philip Kingsley Tricho Complex Supplements

A food supplement designed to maintain healthy hair that contains a mix of vitamins and minerals including the essential amino acid L-Lysine, Pantothenic Acid, Methionine, Iron, Vitamins D3, C & B12 as well as Copper to help your hair combat grey. You take two tablets a day for four months. As this experiment has only been going a month it is early days for me, but I would say I have already noticed an improvement in my nail strength.

Philip Kingsley Tricho Complex *www.philipkingsley.co.uk*

EFFICACY : 5/5 | VALUE FOR MONEY: 3/5

Vitamin C

Trinny takes 6000 mg of Vitamin C a day. The daily recommended dose is 65-90 mg to avoid deficiency. So this is an enormous amount of Vitamin C. She says she takes it to counter the effects of smoking and sugar, which both destroy Vitamin C. I don't smoke or eat a lot of sugar so I took 4000 mg a day. It is water soluble so your body just pees out what you don't use, which I guess is probably quite a lot. It did certainly feel like I had more energy, and according to the experts I spoke to it's great for the immune system. I will certainly keep going with the mega doses, but might reduce it a tad to say 3000 a day because one side effect is that it does have a rather dramatic effect on one's digestive system.

EFFICACY : 5/5 | VALUE FOR MONEY: 5/5

Interim Score!

More than £10,000 a year! Calculation based on one Foreo for £169;

three Black Rose Masks for £286.50, £180 for 3000 mg of Vitamin C a day; £450 for two Philip Kingsley Tricho Complex per day; £660 for one peel every other month; £1000 for two areas of Botox twice a year; £1000 for three Ellipse laser treatments plus one top-up; £600 for four laser facials a year; £1280 for six times roots and tint; £408 for six times full-face and eyebrow threading; £3800 for three vampire facials plus one top up; one Elvie £149; £213 for six times Rudolph Facial Scrub Mask; £227 for one Cherry Lip Patch per week.

There is no doubt that my skin is a lot better than it was when I started. It is clearer, the fine lines are less visible, the larger ones where the Botox has taken effect have more or less vanished, and my age spots are lighter than they were when I started. I fully expect the results to keep improving over the next few weeks. I think the major lesson from my month as Trinny has been two-fold; one if you have unlimited funds (and time) you can dramatically affect the ageing process and two I definitely need to take more time and care over my skin, even if that just means regular home care such as peels, exfoliation and of course daily cleansing morning and night. In fact of the two I would say that regular home care is more important than a monthly laser treatment or Vampire Facial. If you don't look after your skin on a daily basis an expensive treatment now and again won't really help. My advice to those of you who (like me) can't afford regular trips to high-end dermatologists and spas is to invest in some good Botox and focus more on your homecare routine.

Alternatives

Less pricey options include the Clarins Extra Firming Mask (*clarins.com*) which is half the price of the Sisley one. It contains, among other active ingredients, Hyaluronic acid for hydration and promises smoother and more radiant skin in just 10 minutes. It is a fabulous light purple colour and the instructions suggest that you by prepping your skin with a light finger massage before applying it you will help the mask to absorb. My skin looked refreshed and toned after use. Even more of a bargain is the Face Inc by Nails Inc 40 Winks Anti-Ageing Sheet Mask (*www.nailsinc.com*). It contains collagen and multivitmains. The trickiest thing is to find the spare 15 minutes you need for it to take effect. It says firming and brightening on the packet and that is just what it does. Another mid-budget winner is the Esteé Lauder Micro Essence Infusion Mask (*www.esteelauder.co.uk*), which contains the brand's exclusive mix of micronutrients, peptides and ferments and should be left on for ten minutes — it is both deeply nourishing and hydrating.

It is tough to find an alternative to a good hair stylist, but there are options that will help. In terms of root colour, as I did go a shade lighter and you won't need the grey roots covered quite as often. There is also a really good product called Wow Root Cover Up (*www.colorwowhair.com/us/rootcoverup*) that touches up roots in between visits to the salon. You could also try this website that promises bespoke colour online: *ww.esalon.co.uk*.

Sad, mad or really a rather good idea..?

For those of you who thought that injecting poison into one's forehead in order to stay young was wacky enough — think again. As women become increasingly obsessed with flawless complexions and staying wrinkle-free there are more and more weird and wonderful things that supposedly help us to stay young. Sad, mad or are they onto something? Judge for yourself.

Crocodile bath. The ancient Greeks soaked in warm mud baths of crocodile excrement, which they believed could dramatically slow the ageing process. They also used it as a facemask mixed with donkey's milk. Eeeeew!

Dermagenetics — this process uses a swab from the inside your cheek to create a personal anti-ageing formula based on your own DNA. It was developed by a US biosciences company called GeneLink in 2004. The theory behind it is that most cosmetic creams are not suited to our genetic make-up and so the skin can't metabolise them. According to a spokesman at Dermagenetics all over the counter products use the top 10 anti-ageing ingredients to create skin creams and they don't necessarily agree with your skin type. With the swab you send to their lab, Dermagenetics test your genetic propensity for collagen breakdown, wrinkling and overall health. They then create a bespoke formula just for you. The base cream uses, among other things, lavender oil and citrus oil. The genetically selected ingredients include fennel extract, red algae extract and grape extract. Apparently Goldie Hawn, Meg Ryan and Teri Hatcher all use Dermagenetics which may or may not be a recommendation depending on how you think they look.

The Teeter Table, one for bald boys. The good news is there is a cure for baldness that doesn't involve stitches or skin grafts. The bad news is you are strapped to a metal contraption that doesn't look dissimilar to a sophisticated torture instrument and hung upside down. Welcome to the Teeter Table, the latest in anti-ageing technology. The idea is that the blood flows to your scalp, thus stimulating hair follicles to grow. According to a nurse at HB Health in London which has the contraption it is important not to do more than a 20 degree inversion at a time, so you will need to make several visits before you get the full-on effect. The cost? It's complimentary to clients. They're too kind….

Cryotherapy, otherwise known as ice chamber treatment: You are shut in a room where the temperature is minus 130 degrees Celsius for three minutes. Apparently the treatment helps with cellulite, fatigue and minor injuries. That's if you don't die of a heart attack.

Stem cells from umbilical cord tissue — The claim is that foetal tissue from aborted babies is extremely rich in regenerative cells. Basically the new cells act like building blocks, targeting organs that are not functioning and encouraging them to regenerate. There is a debate raging in the US about the treatment. President Bush once called it 'godless' and vetoed any public funding, but California's governor Arnold Schwarzenegger allocated $80 million dollars to research the topic. In the UK stem-cell research is strictly governed and this sort of stem-cell treatment is banned. But you can easily fly to Barbados to the Institute for Regenerative Medicine or the Medra Clinic in the Dominican Republic and for a cost of about £15,000 have stem cells injected into the veins on the back of your hand. The clinic claims you will look and feel different after just a month, although it does not go as far as saying that it will help reduce wrinkles. They say results last up to a year before you need a top-up. Sceptics include Dr Stephen Minger, director of stem-cell biology at King's College London. He claims the treatment could even cause cancer, infection or tumours. He also fears that women are being driven by poverty to have abortions and not electing to abort for more valid reasons. A spokeswoman at the Edinburgh-based Institute for Stem Cell Research says there have been no controlled clinical trials that back the claims of those providing stem-cell treatments and so there is no hard evidence that it works.

Safetox, a contraption made out of a rather garish blue plastic, which can apparently change your life. You wear it on your forehead and it releases electronic impulses via an adhesive patch which relax your muscles and stops you frowning. You wear it for five-minute intervals twice a day over a period of four to six weeks. The elderly (or seriously wrinkly) will have to carry on for a few months. Once the initial treatment period is over you need a top-up of around two five-minute sessions per week. The manufacturers are heralding it as a safe and effective alternative to Botox and the facelift. I don't know if it stops you ageing, but it does make you look like something out of Thunderbirds, which may have its advantages.

Kombucha, the so-called mushroom of life. Fermented extract of mushroom may not seem like the obvious thing to put on your face but according to Dr Miralles, founder of the Global Beauty Anti-ageing range, it has the power to multiply collagen cells thus plumping up the skin and improving its appearance. His creams contain three per cent Kombucha, the only beauty product in the world to do so. But why only put it on your face? In Russia and Eastern Europe people drink Kombucha tea in order to live longer and feel better. According to a spokeswoman at Harvey Nichols which stocks Dr Miralles's Kombucha-based face cream and mask you can not only drink it but use it as a steam treatment by covering your head with a towel and sitting over bowl of steaming Kombucha tea. Maybe you could drink it afterwards, thus completing your internal and external treatment.

Lake Siverskoe, possibly the simplest of all the treatments mentioned. This lake north of Moscow is said to have rejuvenating powers. The legend goes that you just have to splash water from the lake on your face and you stop the ageing process. It couldn't be simpler. A friend of mine was there a few winter's ago and there were scores of women trying to make holes in the ice to get to the magical water. There is no clinical evidence that the water does you any good at all, but legend has it that monks in a nearby monastery have endowed it with rejuvenating powers through the centuries because of their constant praying and purity. Vasily III, Russia's first Tsar obviously believed in its magic, he came here to pray for an heir. Shortly afterwards his wife Elena fell pregnant with the future Ivan the Terrible. Be careful what you wish for.

The Aberdeen Organic Bull Semen Treatment. Yes, the organic bit apparently makes all the difference. This is a treatment for your hair, the idea being that as your hair is made up of protein, some proteins can help form a protective layer around the strands to increase health and lustre.

Leech therapy. Apparently Demi Moore is a devotee of this medieval sounding therapy that involves leeches being placed on your body and sucking your blood.

The Japanese nightingale poo facial. Apparently a favourite with Victoria Beckham. Why the nightingales have to be Japanese I have no idea, but this facial unlocks your inner Geisha beauty…

Vinotherapy. Literally bathing in red wine. You will need around 150 large glasses of plonk to fill a bath. Apparently the antioxidants created in the wine-making process (called polyphenols) are ten times more effective than vitamin E at preventing wrinkles. Red wine of course also contains resveratrol, which has an anti-inflammatory and therefore anti-ageing effect.

Bee venom. There was a rumour a while back that Kate Middleton owes her flawless complexion to bee venom. It has not been confirmed or denied by the palace but of course the magical properties for bees (remember when we all had to start popping royal jelly pills?) cannot be denied.

The placenta face mask. As gross as it sounds but a favourite among celebs who believe the proteins and enzymes in placentas from human or other mammal births are great for your skin.

Ceramic crystal treatment. Pieces of porcelain are injected into your skin to 'hold up' your face and also encourage collagen production.

Tibetan Monk Exercises. Perhaps the least zany of them all. A series of 'five Tibetan rites' that have been dubbed the 'fountain of youth' these yoga-inspired exercises have been practiced daily by Tibetan monks for 2500 years in order to live long, vibrant and healthy lives. They include twists, forward bends and back bends. You do each exercise 21 times. I did try it and it was a bit much so I did 11 of each and am planning to build up. For some reason whatever number you end on, it has to be odd. You don't have to go to Tibet, so this is one you can do at home!

15

Hard truths

'It is not true that people stop pursuing dreams because they grow old,
they grow old because they stop pursuing dreams.'
Gabriel Garcia Marquez

Sophie and I are in our favourite restaurant talking about men. We have known each other for almost 30 years. And it strikes me that the only thing that has really changed is that we don't smoke any more. Ok so we obviously look older to the passer-by than we did when we first met, but we don't feel any older. And after a few glasses of wine we don't look any older to each other. Added to which, our conversation isn't any 'older'. I suppose it helps that Sophie hasn't got married and doesn't have children; so that rules out several 'grown-up' topics of conversation such as stretch marks and school fees.

On a table close to us sit two other women. I haven't really noticed them but at first glance guess they are about 10 years older than us. Sophie motions towards them. 'Don't look now,' she says, 'but isn't that Claire from the year below? Do you remember, she used to do fitness training with us at uni?'

I only went to fitness training once, because I fancied the trainer, and ended up in hospital with a split chin, so no I don't remember Claire but am astounded she was at university during the same decade as me, let alone the year below.

'Why does she look so OLD?' I whisper to Sophie.

'Well, for a start it's the way she dresses.'

I sneak another look. Claire is dressed in a flowery dress with a high collar. Looks like a Laura Ashley type creation. It is shapeless, and so makes her look shapeless too.

'Mind you,' continues Sophie, 'I think she always dressed like that.'

Sophie is wearing skinny jeans, a white silk shirt and leather boots. Her hair is loose, blonde and long. I am dressed in jeans with leather boots too, although mine are not knee-length as Sophie's are. There are certain things a mother of three can't really get away with. I am wearing a polka-dot shirt from Top Shop and a fur gillet. I am having a rare good hair day, having just had my roots done and my hair blow-dried.

Claire's hair is grey at the roots and dragged back in a ponytail. And there is something in the way both women move that set them apart too. It's almost as if Claire has decided that she's a certain age and will therefore look, act and behave a certain age. No such risk with Sophie who is wearing the same sort of clothes she wore when we first met (OK maybe not the micro-mini) and is plotting to seduce a 25 year-old on her art course.

I am not quite as youthful as my friend, but I would certainly never be seen dead with greying roots. Or a Laura Ashley dress come to think of it.

As I watch Claire and her friend walk out of the restaurant I realise that although we all age, it is up to us take control of the ageing process. We need to meet it head on. We have the power to dictate how we want to age, rather than have it foisted upon us. We can decide whether we want to look like middle-aged women or not. At least up to a certain point.

Sophie and my discussion moves (briefly) away from men and onto ageing. She is adamant that with the right diet, exercise and a little outside help we can take full control of how we look as we get older. And she is living proof of that.

One of the key elements to ageing, or rather not ageing, is attitude. Claire's attitude is all wrong. She is putting ten years on her age simply by acting like she thinks a woman of her age ought to. First and foremost by the way she dresses, but also the way she looks and moves, it's almost as if she knows no one will notice her and therefore walks around like someone who is old and invisible. I only saw her briefly but she oozed that 'for me the war is over' kind of attitude. This is not the way forward. We need to meet ageing head on, arms raised for battle, not just keel over and let it happen.

But it's not just about the way we look. The psychological effects of ageing are just as damaging and ageing as our wrinkles. We age prematurely by closing our minds, losing interest and rejecting any inkling of ambition. We literally give up on life, even before it gives up on us. If you put Claire and my friend Sophie in a room next to each other and asked people to guess their age, most would say that Sophie is at least ten years younger if not more. And this is not just because of how they dress, or the grey roots, it's about a state of mind. A belief that they're still in the game, that they still count, that they're not invisible. And who controls our state of mind? We do.

How many times have you heard the expression 'silly old cow' or 'stupid old fool'? The presumption is that as we get older, we become more irritating, more narrow-minded, more, well, stupid. Why is this?

Of course some of it is physical deterioration. 'As we age, brain cell connections become dismantled,' explains Baroness Susan Greenfield, a British scientist who is famous for her research into Alzheimer's and Parkinson's. 'The result of this is that there are lots of things going on that you don't quite understand. So you become like a small child.' But quite often it is not just the result of the physical illness. 'Ageing is always two sides of the same coin. There is no psychological impact that isn't rooted in the physical and vice versa. Amazingly people are saying that physical exercise can help the growth of new brain cells because what you're doing is increasing the blood supply to the brain so the cells are in better shape.'

Professor Greenfield adds that we should remain 'interested and be curious. My mother joined a chess club aged 86. Learn a new language, get into debating.'

And above all, don't stop striving. 'What do you want to be? Why stop stretching yourself just because you're getting older, this is the perfect time to stretch yourself as you never have before.'

Is there a cut-off? A time when we settle into an armchair and say, oh well that's it for me. I'm too old to go to the cinema/fly to Paris/read a book by a cutting-edge author? Why is this? A cop out? Laziness? Fear of failure? I feel very strongly that ageing well is like exercising a muscle, or doing a stretch. The first day you try to touch your toes you think you might keel over, but you keep at it and then one day you can not only touch your toes but get your hands flat on the floor next to them. In the same way, you need to almost fight ageing, or at least fight the pernicious and damaging attitude that you need to do less as you get older. In fact you need to do more!

There is absolutely no reason why getting older means getting more stupid and less successful. History is full of late bloomers who really only flourished when they grew old. Here are a few examples:

Mary Wesley (1912-2003), the novelist. My personal favourite because she gives me hope that I may yet write a bestseller, Mary published her first novel in 1983 at the age of 70. She went on to write 10 novels in total, many of them bestseller and three of them filmed for TV. And this was all in the last 20 years of her life. She was famous for writing about sex, often illicit sex, which was unexpected from a woman of her class and age. 'The young always think that they invented sex and somehow hold full literary rights on the subject,' she once said when questioned about it.

I love her attitude to ageing: 'A lot of people stop short. They don't actually die but they say, 'Right I'm old, and I'm going to retire,' and then they dwindle into nothing. They go off to Florida and become jolly boring.' This is exactly what we have to avoid. Florida is a ghastly place, even when you're young. And again she sums up ageing with attitude so well with the following quote: 'I have no patience with people who grow old at 60 just because they are entitled to a bus pass. Sixty should be the time to start something new, not put your feet up.'

Margot Fonteyn (1919-1991), an English ballerina who is regarded as one of the greatest classical dancers of all time. She was about to hang up her pointe shoes aged 42 when a young Russian dancer called Rudolf Nureyev defected to the west and joined the Royal Ballet. She went on dancing with him until she finally retired at the age of 61. One of their most famous partnerships was Romeo & Juliet, both on stage and film. Yes, a middle-aged woman playing a teenage girl and she was incredible. Rudolf, who was 19 years her junior, said of her: 'At the end of *Lac des Cygnes* when she left the stage in her great white tutu I would have followed her to the end of the world.'

Julia Child (1912-2004), now immortalised in a film starring Meryl Streep, Julia wanted to become a writer but of novels rather than cookbooks. Her first cookbook, written along with two members of a gourmet club she joined aged 36, took her ten years, only to be rejected by publishers. It was finally published when she was 49 and five months later she embarked on a TV career that spanned three decades. At the age of 88 she was awarded the French Legion d'honneur and elected to the American Academy of Arts and Sciences. She said of her decision to take up cooking so late: 'I was thirty-seven years old and still discovering who I was.'

Paul Cézanne (1839-1906), French artist and Post-Impressionist painter. Thanks to a generous allowance from his father he didn't need to work and spent a lot of his adulthood perfecting his technique. Held his first exhibition at the age of 56.

George Eliot (1819-1880), Mary Ann Evans, who wrote under the pseudonym of George Eliot, was 40 when her first novel was published. If that seems old now, back then it was positively ancient. She carried on writing until her death at the age of 61. Her fourth novel, *Middlemarch*, is regarded by many as the greatest novel ever written in the English language.

Philip Rabinowitz (1904-2008), crazy South African runner who made the *Guiness Book of Records* in 2004 for being the fastest ever centenarian to run 100 metres. He made it in 30.86 seconds (the world record is 9.58 seconds, held by someone just a tad younger). He died aged 104 and said the secret to his longevity was walking four miles a day.

And this is of course not limited to famous people. I recently met a woman called Catherine who is 93 years old. I was coming back from a walk, staying at a friend's house in the most idyllic village in the Sussex Hills. I walked past her as she was putting out her recycling bin ready for the morning.

'Are you my new temporary neighbour?' she asked me, smiling and reaching out her hand.

She invited me in for a glass of wine and we sat in her garden talking about everything from colonialism (she had lived in what was then Tanganika, now Tanzania), public schools, local pubs and Edward St Aubyn, a contemporary novelist who has been compared to Evelyn Waugh.

Catherine worked as a pathologist well into her seventies. She speaks French and Italian and chatting to her was just like talking to a friend. I don't know why it surprised me that, for example, she knew exactly who I was talking about when I mentioned Edward St Aubyn, but it did. I felt slightly ashamed that I had underestimated her, but also inspired and hopeful. If Catherine, aged 93, knows who he is then there's hope for us all. I suppose what I mean by that is that life doesn't need to be over, you can still discover and appreciate literature well into your 90s.

So why shouldn't someone over 90 know what's going on in the contemporary literary world? Why do we assume that old people only like old things? And that they are to be pitied, looked after, often ridiculed?

What can be more impressive and brilliant than a woman sitting in her garden having worked in some of the best hospitals of the world, still capable of driving herself around and lugging her bins to the right spot for the fascistic Surrey garbage collectors, sipping white wine?

The fact that she sometimes lost track of our conversation for a minute or two, and that she still refers to herself as 'we' not in the royal sense but obviously referring to her late husband, is irrelevant. This is a woman you can have a better conversation with than many people half her age, and most people a third of her age.

Catherine is full of plans. She is off to Italy soon to improve her Italian. Next week she is going to Bristol to see one of her children. Another great friend of mine is in his eighties. He plays the piano like a pro, has a full head of grey hair and is among the most interesting and captivating people I know. He has half a dozen grandchildren but struts around town like a young stud looking impossibly glamorous.

The lesson I learned from people like Catherine and Peter is that life doesn't have to end when you get old, or even get less interesting. In fact it can get more interesting in many ways. Peter now has the time to travel to meet his children in far-flung places like India, and sit on my terrace redesigning my garden for me, because he doesn't have the pressure of earning money to support anyone any more.

Final word

I may be good at coming up with advice, but I'm not sure how effectively I can follow it myself.

How well you age is up to you. OK so a certain amount is down to genetics. But a lot, some experts estimate around 75 per cent, is down to you. Or rather down to the way you live. You only have to look at the faces of alcoholics, drug addicts or heavy smokers to see how right this is.

Inevitably what we put into our bodies, and how we treat our bodies, is reflected in our appearance.

The two main tools to combat ageing (or at least to meet it head on) are food and exercise. You can spend thousands of pounds a week on expensive face creams, but if you only eat processed food and never move you will still look dreadful. Of course no one wants to hear this. We all want a magical anti-ageing 'cure' that involves no effort. And yes it is a bit more of an effort to cook a soup, rather than buy a tin, and you might very well prefer to sit on the sofa watching someone play tennis rather than play it yourself. But how you live from now on (actually if you remember the Anna Phillips quote from the moment you are conceived) will have an effect on how well you age. It will affect not only how you look, but also how you move, how healthy you are and how well you feel.

We're not talking about seismic changes here. We're talking about walking up stairs as often as you can, about doing half an hour's exercise a day, about chopping up some vegetables for a fresh meal rather than buying a packet.

Of course on top of my two basics I put skincare as an extremely powerful third tool. This encompasses everything from using sunscreen daily to twice daily cleansing to weekly exfoliating to thrice-weekly face masks at home to the monthly facial and active (predominantly natural) products.

I call them the three Ss: Sustenance, sun salutations and skincare. Pretty easy to remember and pretty easy to follow.

If you're not convinced by what you have read why not just try it? For one month commit to living by the three Ss. I'm not saying never have processed food, I sometimes do, I'm not saying you have to exercise every single day, but do more days on than off. Try to eat well more often than not. And definitely cleanse your skin every day, even if you only manage it at night.

If you don't feel and look better I will be amazed. Let me know how you get on.

Acknowledgements

A huge thank you to all the people who have helped me with my research for this book from plastic surgeons to Oxford academics and countless more. Without your time, treatments and patience it would not have been possible to write. Thanks must also go to my publisher Martin Rynja for all his hard work and dedication, and masses of thanks to the diligent and lovely Sarah New. I would also like to thank my great friend Carla McKay who has inspired me to take a more holistic view of ageing, as opposed to relying on skin treatments. I am also grateful to Carla for being older than me, which endlessly cheers me up as I begin to feel like I'm always the oldest person in the room. Finally thanks to my husband Rupert who has put up with my talking about wacky anti-ageing treatments for longer than I can remember and always pretends to believe me when I tell him I haven't had anything done.

Glossary

What is it, what does it do, where do I get it?

Everything you need to know about the anti-ageing products and ingredients out there.

Active ingredients:
Things like green tea, grape seed extract and vitamin C. Ingredients that can have an active effect on your skin, in other words actually make a difference to it as opposed to just moisturise it or make it feel nice.

Advanced Glycation End-products (AGE):
Toxic compounds that form naturally in the body in small amounts, but are present in large quantities in many of the foods we consume. Scientifically speaking, they are lipids or proteins that glycate after being exposed to sugars. They have been linked to more diseases and health problems than any other single dietary component, such as but not limited to skin ageing, heart and kidney disease, dementia and Alzheimer's.

Amino Peptides:
When chains of collagens break down into small strands, these

linked pieces of amino acids are called peptides. Though no longer part of the collagen, they are still active molecules that can signal the skin to make more collagen. Amino-peptides are shown to have a remarkable anti-inflammatory effect deep within the skin's surface that promotes anti-ageing properties, including tissue regeneration.

Antioxidants (vitamin C and E):
These help protect healthy cells from damage by free radicals. Vitamin E protects from cell damage that can lead to cataracts, cancer and heart disease and some chronic diseases. Vitamin C protects from infection and damage in body cells, helps to produce collagen, keeps blood vessels and capillary walls firm and aids in the absorption of folate and iron.

Blepharoplasty (eye lift):
Surgery to eliminate sagging of skin from upper and lower eyelids. It involves removing excess skin from eyelids, smoothing the muscles underneath, and repositioning the excess fat in the area of the lower eyelid that meets the cheek, so that this area is smooth. Usually incisions are made on the natural creases of the upper and lower lids so that the scars are not noticeable. It typically takes between one and three hours and any swelling and bruising from surgery should be gone in one to two weeks. Final results will become apparent in several months. This surgery can also be done with a laser rather than a scalpel, in which case the procedure can be done alongside laser eyelid rejuvenation.

Botox:
A toxic protein (Botulinum) that paralyses muscles and therefore temporarily erases or significantly decreases wrinkles. Botox injections paralyse the muscles, preventing wrinkle formation. Results are seen within a few days of the treatment and typically

last from three to six months. Any drooping or bruising is a result of the application of the injection rather than the toxin itself. Side effects should wear off within six weeks. Botox can be administered by a variety of practitioners including dermatologists, plastic surgeons, aesthetic spa physicians, dentists, nurse practitioners, nurses and physician assistants. Be sure that you go to a professional who knows what they're doing.

Botulinum toxin:
Also known as Botox. It is a protein and neurotoxin produced by a certain type of bacteria. It is the most toxic substance known, so just a small dose could lead to botulism, a potentially fatal paralytic illness. However, the tiny doses of the toxin in Botox injections are of course not enough to cause these effects. In the 1950s, doctors found that tiny injections of the toxin could be used for medical purposes, as they decreased muscle activity. It was therefore primarily used to treat various types of spasms, but was developed for cosmetic use in the 1990s.

Ceramides:
Lipids that are part of the main barrier of the skin and make up most of the layer which holds the skin cells together. A low level of ceramides can cause eczema, which can be healed by topical replacement preparations. They can be used in anti-ageing products to plump up skin.

Chemical/acid peels:
This skin treatment uses a chemical product that causes dead skin to peel off and the skin underneath to heal, promoting smoother skin and reducing the appearance of wrinkles and scars. Alpha hydroxy acid (AHA) and beta hydroxy acid (BHA) are probably the most common acids used for chemical peels. AHAs are naturally occurring and are the mildest of acid peels; they are not

highly effective for wrinkles beyond fine lines. BHAs are better able to penetrate deeper into the pores than AHAs, so are becoming more commonly used. They are also beneficial in face washes or creams in smaller amounts as part of a daily skincare regimen. Deeper peels, such as the retinoic acid peel, can remove scars, wrinkles and pigmentation problems, but require professional application and several days of peeling for effect. All types of peels are usually applied in a medical office, but stronger peels in particular, as there is more risk the deeper the acid is able to penetrate the skin.

AHAs — Alpha hydroxy acids are chemical compounds, either synthetic or natural, that reduce wrinkles and the signs of ageing by improving the overall look and feel of skin. Lactic acid is found in sour milk and tomato juice. There are five usual fruit acids: citric acid, glycolic acid, lactic acid, malic acid and tartaric acid. They can be found in some creams and chemical peels.

BHAs — Beta hydroxyl acid is also known as salicylic acid. It works as an exfoliant, causing cells in the epidermis to fall away and make room for new skin to grow anew. It is only lipid soluble, so it can get inside pores, unlike substances that are water soluble.

Jessner's peel — A chemical peel, like an AHA or BHA that does not penetrate as deeply. It was originally known as the Coombe's formula. The acid percentages are so mild, however, that much less peeling takes place and therefore it will not have an effect on more severe cases of wrinkles, pigmentation, etc. It is often used as a 'before' treatment for retinoic acid peels (definition below) to help open up the skin so the stronger peel can penetrate deeper.

Phenol chemical peel — The strongest of all the chemical peels, for those with pronounced wrinkles, blotches or sun-damaged skin. The active ingredient is croton oil, which causes intense and caustic exfoliation in the skin. The regeneration of the dermal architecture is stimulated to restore the younger dermis to a level beyond that of more superficial peels.

Retinoic acid peel — A chemical peel that goes deeper than either an AHA or a BHA to remove scars, wrinkles and pigmentations problems. It requires professional application, and the client leaves the dermatologist with the peel still on their skin. It may be washed off four to six hours later.

Coenzyme Q10:
Also known as ubiquinone and ubidecarenone. It is similar to a vitamin and used to produce energy for cell maintenance and growth. It also works as an antioxidant and helps to protect skeletal and heart muscles.

Collagen:
A type of protein that connects our bodily tissues and provides the skin with strength, flexibility, and resilience. It is constantly being produced to help the skin smooth out and stay firm. However, collagen production begins to slow as early as our mid-20s. Collagen, and 'mini collagens' like amino peptides are often put into skin creams to help revitalize collagen production as we age, however there is a chance that such creams will actually have no effect. Skin creams sometimes cause the collagen to break down too much to be useful, and they sometimes have difficulty penetrating the upper layers of the skin.

Controlled damage:
Controlled damage is a way of stimulating collagen production through for example peels and lasers so that the collagen will not only heal the controlled damage but wrinkles and scars on the skin as well.

Curcuminoids (turmeric):
A major component of turmeric that is an aid for anti-inflammation, anti-tumour and antioxidant properties. However,

curcuminoids are insoluble in water and therefore do not usually break down into particles small enough to be absorbed through the intestinal wall and into the bloodstream. It is best eaten with food, in such dishes as curries. There are many recipes that include turmeric from regions of South and Southeast Asia and the Middle East, but it can be used as a supplement for black pepper in some dishes for a little extra kick.

Face and neck lifts:
For the face, the surgeon makes an incision from behind the ear, under the earlobe, and up to the temples. Then the skin is lifted as the muscle and tissue underneath are adjusted. Sometimes fat and/or excess skin is removed. The incision lines are made in a place of the skin's natural crease so they will be less apparent. The incision is then closed with stitches or metal clips. Usually takes two to four hours. Neck lifts may include removing excess skin or fat, injecting with Botox, and removing or altering neck muscles.

Fibroblasts:
A type of cell that makes collagen and the extracellular matrix, the main connective tissue cells in the body and play a vital role in tissue repair. In their less active state, known as fibrocyte, they are responsible for tissue maintenance and metabolism.

Fractional CO2 laser skin resurfacing:
Removes microscopic areas of tissue deep in the dermis and on skin's surface, leaving areas of skin untouched to help skin regenerate. It can be used for wrinkles and discoloration, scars from acne, burns, etc. Treatment takes from three to four hours and patients will be given twilight anesthesia (where the patient is sedated but not unconscious) or anesthesia injections. Patients may experience redness, swelling, slight crusting and oozing in first week after treatment. Skin may appear slightly pink for two

weeks afterwards but can be covered up with make-up.

Fraxel laser:
Technology used to help fix fine lines and wrinkles, surface scarring, pigmentation and sun damage. The laser uses thousands of microscopic laser columns that are each only one-tenth the diameter of a single hair follicle to treat small areas of skin at a time. They penetrate the top layers of skin and stimulate collagen production while resurfacing the skin. It works best with focused concerns such as hands, and is not a total skin makeover. Since it works with natural skin cells, best results are after one to five treatments and the results take one to three weeks to show.

Hair transplants:
Various techniques have been around for years, but the latest are only just being released to the general public now. The NeoGraft procedure, for example, is the first FDA approved follicular unit harvesting and implantation system. Instead of needing to remove a large strip from the back of the scalp, as with old procedures, NeoGraft utilizes a targeted removal of individual hair follicles for a minimally-invasive procedure. It allows for a more precise and natural looking hairline, reduces the necessary recovery time and practically eliminates scarring.

Hand and neck rejuvenation:
For hands, filler can be injected into hands to make them look younger and plumper, filling in the dips between the bones. Results typically last one to two years. The neck can be Botoxed by placing multiple injections into the lower jawline and the side of the neck to define the jawline and rebalance underlying muscles. Vertical bands and lines can also be removed with a procedure that makes small incisions under the chin or behind the ears to tighten the neck muscles, called platysmaplasty. It is

possible to get neck lift without facelift, although the procedure is painful.

Human growth hormone:
Produced both naturally and synthetically. In the body, it is made in the pituitary gland and spurs growth and regulates many functions for the muscles, bones and heart. However, HGH levels naturally decrease in age, so anti-ageing experts are currently researching whether synthetic injections could reverse or slow down the effects of ageing.

Hyaluronic acid:
Naturally occurs in our bodies, it plays a big role in cell proliferation and movement. The average person has around 15 grams in his or her body, one third of which is renewed every day. When skin is sunburned/exposed to UVB rays, skin cells stop creating as much hyaluronic acid.

Contrary to some claims, hyaluronic acid has no effect at all when used topically in for example a cream but needs to penetrate the upper dermis to have an effect, so there is no point in buying an expensive cream with hyaluronic acid in it. This collagen replacement is made out of natural or synthetic substances. It is administered via injection into the skin to 'fill out' soft tissues, such as creases, folds and wrinkles. These effects typically last up to six months to a year. Major brands include Juvederm, Restylane and Sculptra. Juvederm is a gel, and also the only hyaluronic acid type that is approved by the FDA to last up to one year. Restylane treatments can be repeated once or twice a year, and results can be seen immediately. Sculptra gives more subtle results, but lasts up to two years. An alternative is fat transfer, which uses the body's surplus fat instead of synthetic filler. Though there are potentially perks of stem cell transfer and skin rejuvenation, the results can take weeks to appear.

Laser treatments:

Laser skin resurfacing treatments are used to reduce wrinkles, acne scars, and other skin irregularities, including sun damage and other pigmentation problems. It uses a specially made thermal energy beam that works deep within skin layers to help it naturally repair and reform. It can be used on targeted areas or larger surface areas. There are many different types of laser treatments that are recommended for different concerns. The most common types are CO_2 and erbium lasers, both of which vaporise damaged skin cells at the surface of the skin.

Light therapy for wrinkles:

Red light wavelengths are used to try to improve skin's ability to retain healing elements, thus improving the skin's barrier functions. The light may also stimulate collagen production and reduce the production of a type of pro-inflammatory substances from skin's glands that may contribute to acne. Although there are at-home devices, it is recommended that this treatment be done in a dermatologist's clinic so that the right level of intensity can be achieved.

Light treatments:

Done by dermatologists using UVA or UVB light. Narrow band UVB light is becoming more common, since it avoids the more harmful wavelengths and it also is more intensive than broad spectrum UVB, so treatment times are shorter. It is often used to treat skin conditions such as acne vulgaris, eczema and psoriasis, as well as sleep disorders and some psychiatric conditions.

Linoleic/ linolenic acids/ phospholipids:

Linoleic acid is an essential fatty oil found in the cell membrane's lipids. When applied topically to the skin, it can act as an anti-inflammatory, an acne reducer and help moisture retention.

Liposuction and fat transfer:
A type of cosmetic surgery that breaks up and sucks out unwanted fat from parts of the body through a tube that is inserted under the skin and applied to a high pressure vacuum. It is not a treatment for obesity, and it does not remove cellulite, dimples, or stretch marks. Although the treatment removes fat cells, the patient must maintain a healthy lifestyle in order to maintain their body contour because the remaining fat cells can grow larger. The fat that is removed through liposuction can be transferred to other parts of the body that the patient wishes to augment, such as the breasts or buttocks.

Lycopene:
An antioxidant found mainly in tomatoes, but also in fruits and vegetables with red pigmentation. It benefits the blood vessels around the heart and can help protect against cardiovascular disease and cancer. The best way to deliver it to body tissues is through foods such as tomatoes, watermelon, grapefruit and apricots. It is most effective when cooked, so tomato puree for example is ideal.

Mesotherapy:
An injection that stimulates the middle layer of skin (mesoderm). It works in a variety of applications, such as cellulite and fat reduction and skin rejuvenation. For the skin, it uses a combination of minerals, antioxidants and vitamins to rehydrate and tighten.

Niacinamide:
Also known as nicotinic acid and vitamin B3. It is a powerful cell-communicating ingredient that can improve the skin's elasticity,

erase discolorations, rejuvenate tone and texture and enhance barrier functions.

Pentapeptides:
Amino acids that renew the skin's outermost layer to reveal smoother, younger-looking skin. Pentapeptides work by stimulating the production of new collagen, which helps diminish the appearance of fine lines and wrinkles.

Peptides:
Peptides are strings of amino acids linked by peptide bonds, and they are the building blocks of proteins in your skin. When attached in long chains, they form proteins, but in short chains, they are able to penetrate the top layer skin and communicate with our cells, giving them instructions , for example to create collagen. Their biggest use in anti-ageing products is to stimulate collagen production, as it is the body's natural way of repairing skin cells. Peptides are best used when applied in creams or serum over long periods of time, as they take time to work. Results will appear in four to twelve weeks, and continued use is necessary for results to be maintained.

Rapamycin:
Also known as sirolimus. In the past, it has been given to organ transplant recipients to keep their immune system from rejecting the foreign material, thanks to its ability to repress the immune system. Research is being done to see if it can extend lifespan and influence the effects of ageing.

Resveratrol:
A naturally occurring compound in some plants, especially the roots of Japanese knotweed and grapes. It is produced when the plant is under attack from pathogens such as bacteria or fungi.

Although research on it is ongoing and it is unclear what benefits it may have to humans, it has been found to lengthen the lifespan of model organisms such as rats. In food, it is found in red wine, red grapes, peanuts (especially sprouted), mulberry fruit, and cocoa powder/baking chocolate/dark chocolate. It is known for its antioxidant properties, so may reduce effects of premature skin ageing caused by UV radiation/sun damage. Vino Vera is a range of anti-ageing products based around resveratrol.

Retinol:
A derivative of vitamin A. It improves collagen-depleted skin by lessening the appearance of wrinkles and lines while also augmenting the natural process by which skin reduces the appearance of pore size.

Sirtuins:
A class of proteins that regulate critical biological pathways. It influences ageing and stress resistance and also affects energy efficiency. It can mimic the effects of caloric restriction and is currently being studied for potential life-extending qualities.

SPF:
Sun protection factor is a number on a scale that rates a sunscreen's degree of protection. It does not shield your skin, however, but rather notes how much longer it will take for your skin to redden than unshielded skin. (15 SPF will take 15 times longer, etc.) Not all sunscreen is the same, however, as not all of it protects against both kinds of sun rays: UVA (ultraviolet long-wave) and UVB (ultraviolet short-rays). UVA accounts for about 95% of the radiation on earth, and plays a major part in skin wrinkling and ageing. It is less intensive than UVB, but penetrates the skin deeper. UVB, though less prevalent, is the chief cause of reddening and sunburn, as well as skin damage. Therefore, it is

important that a sunscreen above SPF 15 is used for coverage against both types, to make sure the power is effective, preferably with some combination of ingredients such as zinc oxide, stabilized avobenzone, titanium dioxide, ecamsule and oxybenzone. There are sunscreens that will say they offer multi spectrum protection, however these types of phrases offer no direct correlation with how much protection they offer unless the above ingredients are involved.

Stem Cell anti-ageing treatment:
Uses patient's own stem cells. Stem cells are removed from patient, activated, and multiplied. Then they are reintroduced into the patient's body. They promote growth of certain types of tissue. Fine lines, age spots, wrinkles, etc. may disappear when stem cells are inserted into those areas, as they promote new collagen and tissue.

Topical:
A treatment that is applied to your skin surface, as opposed to an injection or a consumable substance. This includes creams, gels and lotions, which are absorbed into the body through the skin layers.

The Vampire Facial:
Also known as Platelet Rich Plasma (PRP). It uses your own blood to create concentrated platelets and tissue building elements that will be reintroduced to your body via an injection or topically. It will stimulate the regrowth of collagens and help the skin retighten. It is an all natural process to combat sun damage, deep wrinkles, acne scars and pitting and stress marks.